THE
Christmas Carols
BOOK

ISBN 978-0-634-04875-3

HAL•LEONARD®
CORPORATION
7777 W. BLUEMOUND RD. P.O. BOX 13819 MILWAUKEE, WI 53213

Visit Hal Leonard Online at
www.halleonard.com

THE Christmas Carols BOOK

STRUM AND PICK PATTERNS

This chart contains the suggested strum and pick patterns that are referred to by number at the beginning of each song in this book. The symbols ⊓ and ∨ in the strum patterns refer to down and up strokes, respectively. The letters in the pick patterns indicate which right-hand fingers plays which strings.

p = thumb
i = index finger
m = middle finger
a = ring finger

For example; Pick Pattern 2
is played: thumb - index - middle - ring

Strum Patterns   ## Pick Patterns

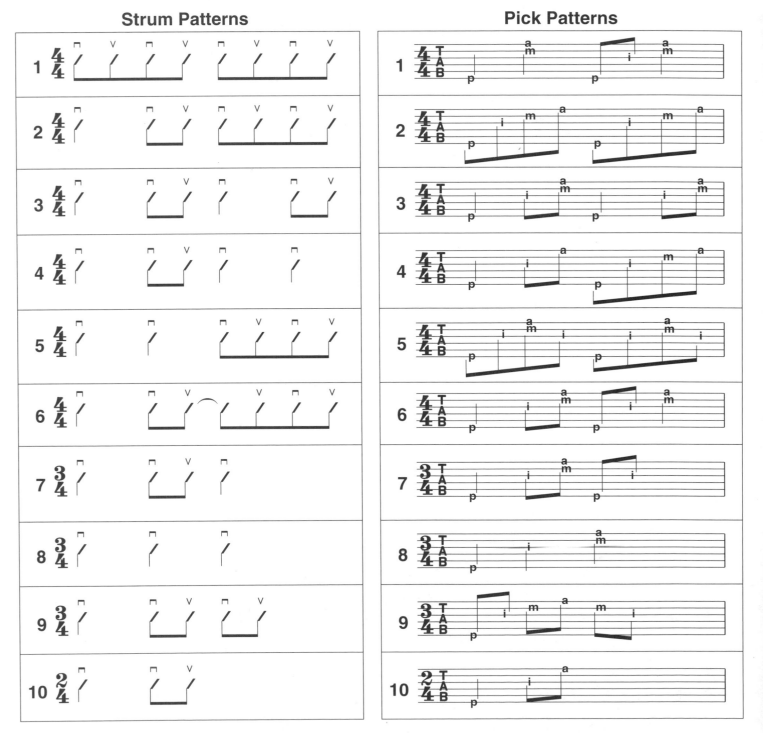

You can use the 3/4 Strum or Pick Patterns in songs written in compound meter (6/8, 9/8, 12/8, etc.).
For example, you can accompany a song in 6/8 by playing the 3/4 pattern twice in each measure.
The 4/4 Strum and Pick Patterns can be used for songs written in cut time (¢) by doubling the note time values in the patterns. Each pattern would therefore last two measures in cut time.

All My Heart This Night Rejoices

Words and Music by Johann Ebeling and Catherine Winkworth

Strum Pattern: 4
Pick Pattern: 3

Verse
Moderately

1. All my heart this night re - joi - ces as I hear far and near,
2. Hark! a voice from yon - der man - ger, soft and sweet doth en - treat.
3. Come, then let us has - ten yon - der. Here let all, great and small,

sweet - est an - gel voi - ces. "Christ is born," their choirs are sing - ing,
"Flee from woe and dan - ger. Breth - ren come from all that grieves you,
kneel in awe and won - der. Love Him who with love is yearn - ing.

'til the air ev - 'ry - where, now with joy is ring - ing. burn - ing!
you are freed. All you need I will sure - ly give you."
Hail the star that from far bright with hope is

Copyright © 2002 by HAL LEONARD CORPORATION
International Copyright Secured   All Rights Reserved

As Each Happy Christmas

Traditional

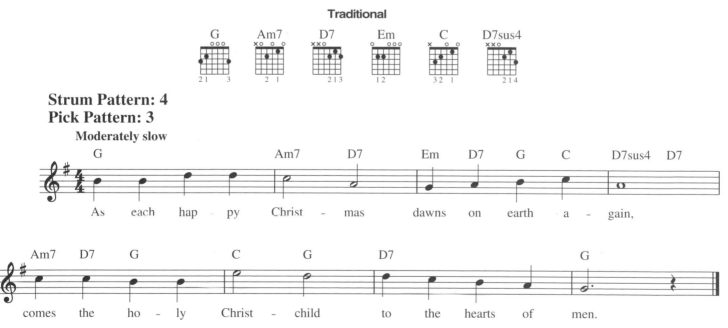

Strum Pattern: 4
Pick Pattern: 3

Moderately slow

As each hap - py Christ - mas dawns on earth a - gain,

comes the ho - ly Christ - child to the hearts of men.

Copyright © 2002 by HAL LEONARD CORPORATION
International Copyright Secured All Rights Reserved

5

Angels From the Realms of Glory

Words by James Montgomery
Music by Henry T. Smart

Strum Pattern: 3
Pick Pattern: 5

Verse
Joyfully

1. An - gels from the realms of glo - ry, wing your flight o'er all the earth.
2., 3., 4. *See additional lyrics*

Ye who sang cre - a - tion's sto - ry, now pro - claim Mes - si - ah's birth.

Chorus

Come and wor - ship! Come and wor - ship! Wor - ship Christ the new - born King! new - born King!

Additional Lyrics

2. Shepherds in the fields abiding,
   Watching o'er your flocks by night,
   God with men is now residing,
   Yonder shines the infant light.

3. Sages, leave your contemplations,
   Brighter visions beam afar;
   Seek the great Desire of Nations;
   Ye have seen His natal star.

4. Saints, before the altar bending,
   Watching long in hope and fear,
   Suddenly the Lord, descending,
   In His temple shall appear.

Angels We Have Heard on High

Traditional French Carol

Translated by James Chadwick

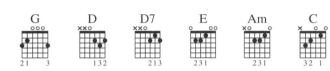

Strum Pattern: 6
Pick Pattern: 6

Additional Lyrics

2. Shepherds, why this jubilee,
   Why your joyous strains prolong?
   What the gladsome tidings be
   Which inspire your heavenly song?

3. Come to Bethlehem and see
   Him whose birth the angels sing;
   Come, adore on bended knee
   Christ the Lord, the newborn King.

4. See within a manger laid
   Jesus, Lord of heaven and earth!
   Mary, Joseph, lend your aid,
   With us sing our Savior's birth.

As With Gladness Men of Old

Words by William Chatterton Dix
Music by Conrad Kocher

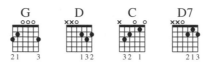

Strum Pattern: 4
Pick Pattern: 5

Additional Lyrics

2. As with joyful steps they sped,
   To that lowly manger bed,
   There to bend the knee before
   Him who Heaven and Earth adore,
   So may we with willing feet
   Ever seek thy mercy seat.

3. As they offered gifts most rare
   At that manger rude and bare,
   So may we with holy joy,
   Pure and free from sin's alloy,
   All our costliest treasures bring,
   Christ, to Thee, our heavenly King.

4. Holy Jesus, every day
   Keep us in the narrow way;
   And, when earthly things are past,
   Bring our ransomed souls at last
   Where they need no star to guide,
   Where no clouds Thy glory hide.

At the Gates of Heaven Above

Traditional Romanian Carol

Additional Lyrics

2. At the gates of heaven above,
   Mary the Mother mild is sitting,
   Holding the Babe, her dearest love.

3. At the gates of heaven above,
   Her tiny Child is weeping sadly,
   Weeping is Christ, her dearest love.

4. At the gates of heaven above,
   "Hush, precious Son, I've gifts to give you,
   Gifts for the Christ, my dearest love."

Away in a Manger

Traditional
Words by John T. McFarland (v.3)
Music by James R. Murray

Additional Lyrics

2. The cattle are lowing, the Baby awakes,
   But little Lord Jesus, no crying He makes.
   I love Thee, Lord Jesus, look down from the sky
   And stay by my cradle 'til morning is nigh.

3. Be near me, Lord Jesus, I ask Thee to stay
   Close by me forever, and love me, I pray.
   Bless all the dear children in Thy tender care,
   And fit us for heaven to live with Thee there.

A Babe Is Born in Bethlehem

Translated by Philip Schaff
Music by Ludvig Lindeman

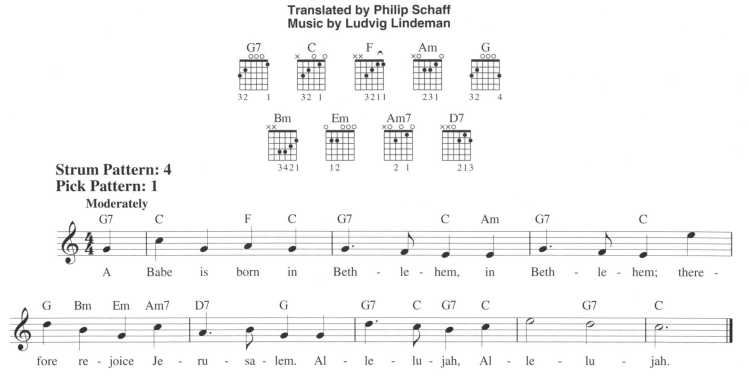

Strum Pattern: 4
Pick Pattern: 1

Moderately

A Babe is born in Beth - le - hem, in Beth - le - hem; there - fore re - joice Je - ru - sa - lem. Al - le - lu - jah, Al - le - lu - jah.

Beside Thy Cradle Here I Stand

Words by Paul Gerhardt
Translated by John Troutbeck
Music from the Geistliche Gesangbuch
Harmonized by J.S. Bach

Strum Pattern: 3, 4
Pick Pattern: 3, 4

Moderately

Be - side Thy cra - dle here I stand, O Thou that ev - er liv - est. And

Outro

bring Thee with a will - ing hand the ver - y gifts Thou giv - est. Ac - cept me, 'tis my

mind and heart, my soul, my strength, my ev - 'ry part that Thou from me de - sir - est.

A Baby in the Cradle

By D.G. Corner

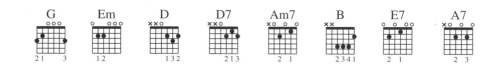

Strum Pattern: 7
Pick Pattern: 7

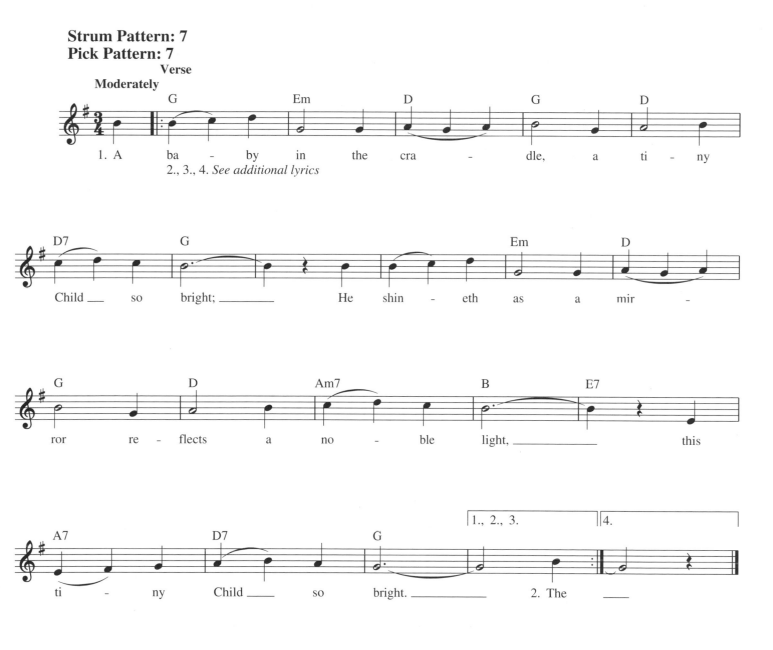

Additional Lyrics

2. The Child of whom we're speaking
   Is Jesus Christ, the Lord;
   He brings us peace and brotherhood
   If we but heed His word,
   Doth Jesus Christ, the Lord.

3. And he who rocks the cradle
   Of the sweet Child so fine
   Must serve with joy and heartiness,
   Be humble and be kind,
   For Mary's Child so fine.

4. O Jesus, dearest Savior,
   Although Thou art so small,
   With Thy great love o'erflowing
   Come flooding through my soul,
   Thou lovely Babe so small.

Baloo, Lammy

17th Century Scottish Melody

Strum Pattern: 7
Pick Pattern: 7

1. This day to you is born a Child, of
2., 3. *See additional lyrics*

Ma - ry meek, the Vir - gin mild; that bless - ed

Bairn so lov - ing and kind, shall now sing prais - es both

heart and mind; Ba - loo, Lam - my. 2. And my.

Additional Lyrics

2. And now shall Mary's little Babe,
For ever be our hope and joy;
Eternal be His reign on earth,
Rejoice, then all people, for this holy birth;
Baloo, Lammy.

3. Sleep soundly, King Jesus, and know no fear,
Thy subjects adoring, watch over Thee here,
God's angels and shepherds, and kine in their stall,
And wise men and Virgin Thy guardians all;
Baloo, Lammy.

Bells Over Bethlehem

Traditional Andalucian Carol

Strum Pattern: 3
Pick Pattern: 4

Verse
Moderately

1. Bells o - ver Beth - le - hem peal - ing, God's sa - cred pres - ence re - veal - ing!
2. *See additional lyrics*

There in the man - ger is rest - ing Je - sus, the earth's rich - est bless - ing! The

Chorus

bells, the bells of Beth - le - hem are ring-ing out the ti - dings, "Good will to all men!"

Bridge

Leave your sheep and come, O shep - herds, pres - ents bring the Child so low - ly,

bring some cheese and bring some wine, for the Moth - er Ma - ry ho - ly. The

Chorus

bells, the bells of Beth - le - hem are ring-ing out the tid - ings, "Good will to all men!" men."

Additional Lyrics

2. Shepherds if you but will hasten,
   Mary, the Blessed Virgin,
   May grant that you may be keeping
   Watch o'er the dear Baby sleeping.

A Boy Is Born in Bethlehem

Traditional

Strum Pattern: 7, 8
Pick Pattern: 7, 8

Moderately

A Boy is born in Beth - le - hem, al - le - lu - ja! And joy is

in Je - ru - sa - lem, al - le - lu - ja, al - le - lu - jah!

A Child Is Born in Bethlehem

14th Century Latin Text adapted by Nicolai F.S. Grundtvig
Traditional Danish Melody

Strum Pattern: 4
Pick Pattern: 3

Verse
Moderately

1. A Child is born in Beth - le - hem, in Beth - le - hem; and joy is in Je -
2., 3., 4. *See additional lyrics*

ru - sa - lem. Al - le - lu - ia, al - le - lu - ia! 2. A ia!

Additional Lyrics

2. A lowly maiden all alone,
So all alone,
Gave birth to God's own Holy Son.
Alleluia, alleluia!

3. She chose a manger for His bed,
For Jesus' bed.
God's angels sang for joy o'erhead,
Alleluia, alleluia!

4. Give thanks and praise eternally,
Eternally,
To God, the Holy Trinity.
Alleluia, alleluia!

Break Forth, O Beauteous, Heavenly Light

Words by Johann Rist
Translated by John Troutbeck
Melody by Johann Schop
Arranged by J.S. Bach

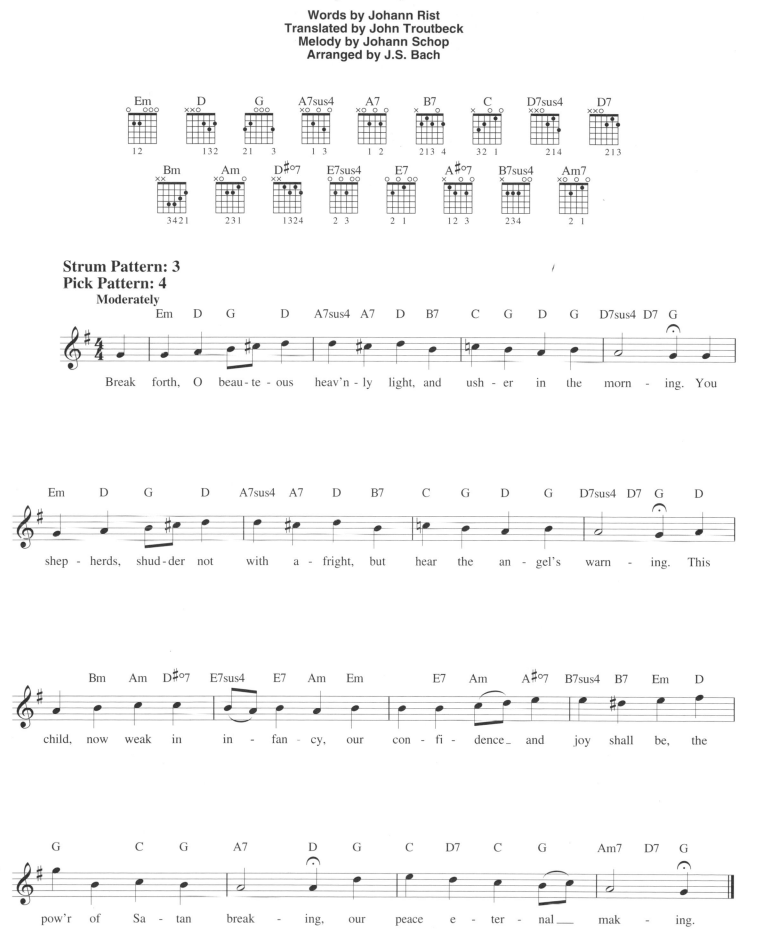

Strum Pattern: 3
Pick Pattern: 4

Moderately

Break forth, O beau-te-ous heav'n-ly light, and ush-er in the morn-ing. You

shep-herds, shud-der not with a-fright, but hear the an-gel's warn-ing. This

child, now weak in in-fan-cy, our con-fi-dence and joy shall be, the

pow'r of Sa-tan break-ing, our peace e-ter-nal mak-ing.

Bring a Torch, Jeannette, Isabella

17th Century French Provencal Carol

Strum Pattern: 7, 9
Pick Pattern: 8, 7

Additional Lyrics

2. Hasten now, good folk of the village,
   Hasten now, the Christ Child to see.
   You will find Him asleep in a manger,
   Quitely come and whisper softly.
   Hush, hush, peacefully now He slumbers,
   Hush, hush, peacefully now He sleeps.

Carol of the Bagpipers

Traditional Sicilian Carol

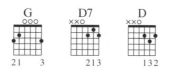

Strum Pattern: 8
Pick Pattern: 8

Moderately

When Christ our Lord was born ____ at Beth - le - hem ____ a -

far, ____ al - though 'twas night, there shone ____ as ____ bright as noon, a

star. Nev - er so bright - ly nev - er so white - ly, shone ____ the

stars, ____ as on ____ that night! The bright - est star ____ went a -

way to call the wise ____ men ____ from the o - ri - ent. ____

Child Jesus

Words by Hans Christian Andersen
Music by Niels Gade

Strum Pattern: 4
Pick Pattern: 3

Verse
Moderately

1. Child Je - sus in a man - ger lay, yet heav - en was His own._____ His
2. *See additional lyrics*

low - ly pil - low was of straw, and 'round Him no light shone._____ But

heav - en sent a star so bright, and ox - en kissed his feet that night. Al -

le - lu - ia, al - le - lu - ia, al - le - lu - ia! 2. O ia!

Additional Lyrics

2. O crippled soul be glad today,
   Cast out your bitter pain.
   His lowly pillow was of straw,
   And 'round Him no light shone.
   But heaven sent a star so bright,
   And oxen kissed His feet that night.
   Alleluia, alleluia, alleluia!

Christ Is Born This Evening

Traditional

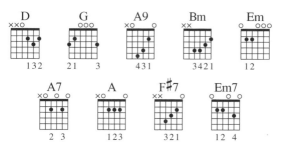

Strum Pattern: 3, 4
Pick Pattern: 4, 5

Verse
Moderately slow

1. Christ is born this eve - ning, let us go re - joic - ing! Though the night is gloom - y,
2. *See additional lyrics*

day will soon be dawn - ing! An - gels from on high are sing - ing to the One who

comes from heav - en: "Glo - ri - a, glo - ri - a, glo - ri - a, in ex - cel - sis De - o!"

An - gels from on high are sing - ing to the One who comes from heav - en: "Glo - ri - a,

glo - ri - a, glo - ri - a, in ex - cel - sis De - o!" o!

Additional Lyrics

2. Shepherds, hasten yonder,
Where the Babe most holy,
In this cold December,
Lies in manger lowly,
See, the star on high is gleaming,
O'er the lovely infant beaming!
Gloria, gloria, gloria,
In excelsis Deo!
See, the star on high is gleaming,
O'er the lovely Infant beaming!
Gloria, gloria, gloria,
In excelsis Deo!

Christit Was Born on Christmas Day

Traditional

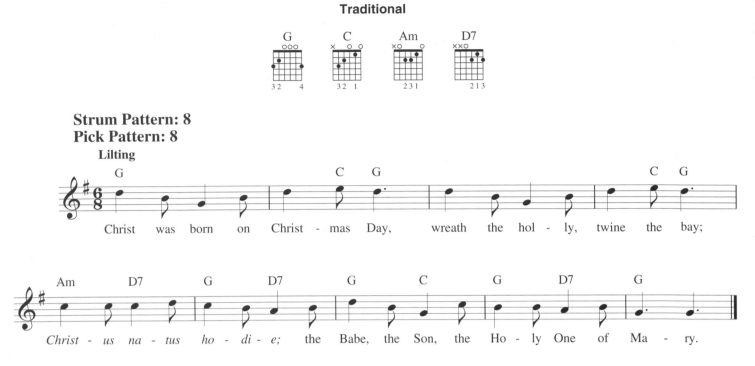

Strum Pattern: 8
Pick Pattern: 8

Lilting

Christ was born on Christ - mas Day, wreath the hol - ly, twine the bay;

Christ - us na - tus ho - di - e; the Babe, the Son, the Ho - ly One of Ma - ry.

Come, All Ye Shepherds

Traditional Czech Text
Traditional Moravian Melody

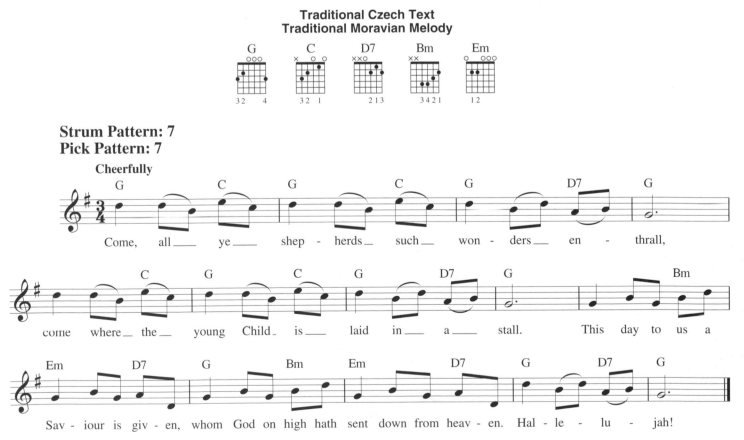

Strum Pattern: 7
Pick Pattern: 7

Cheerfully

Come, all ye shep - herds such won - ders en - thrall,

come where the young Child is laid in a stall. This day to us a

Sav - iour is giv - en, whom God on high hath sent down from heav - en. Hal - le - lu - jah!

Come, All Ye Children

Traditional 17th Century Castilian Melody

Strum Pattern: 8
Pick Pattern: 8

Verse
Moderately

1. Come, all ye chil - dren, your voic - es raise on this morn, on this morn,
2., 3. *See additional lyrics*

bring the glad tid - ings to men that Je - sus was born. Oh! Re - joice! Sweet - ly pro - long what the

an - gels pro - claim, lift up your voic - es, ac - cent their re - frains,

sing, for Christ's birth will bring peace and joy to the earth.___ King!___

Additional Lyrics

2. Wake, all ye children, your Savior was born this night, born this night,
Follow the star for its beam sends forth a bright light.
Oh! Harken!
Angelic choirs tell in sweet words of love,
How the dear God sent his Son from above,
How Jesus' birth will redeem all men upon earth.

3. Rise, all ye children, a lovely day is dawning, is dawning,
Rouse from your slumbers and greet this Christmas morning.
Oh! Laud God!
Sing loud, sing well, 'tis the day of Christ's birth,
While mortals slept, He descended to earth.
Come, let us sing, for we know that Christ is our King!

Come, Thou Long Expected Jesus

Words by Charles Wesley
Music adapted by Henry J. Gauntlett

Strum Pattern: 8
Pick Pattern: 8

Verse
Moderately

1. Come, Thou long - ex - pect - ed Je - sus, born to
2. *See additional lyrics*

set Thy peo - ple free, from our fears _____ and

sins re - lease ____ us, let us find our rest ____ in Thee.

Is - rael's strength ___ and con - so - la - tion, hope of all _____ the

earth ____ Thou art; dear ____ de - sire ____ of ev - 'ry

na - tion, joy of ev - 'ry long - ing heart. throne.

Additional Lyrics

2. Born Thy people to deliver,
   Born a child and yet a king.
   Born to reign in us forever,
   Now Thy gracious kingdom bring.
   By Thine own eternal Spirit
   Rule in all our hearts alone;
   By Thine all sufficient merit,
   Raise us to Thy glorious throne.

Companions, All Sing Loudly

Traditional Basque Carol

Strum Pattern: 3, 4
Pick Pattern: 1, 3

Verse
Moderately

1. Com - pan - ions, all sing loud - ly in praise of ___ Ma - ry dear. Look
2., 3. *See additional lyrics*

up and bear each proud - ly, the day of days is near. On

high ___ 'twas told ___ this sto - ry, that Ma - ry but ___ a maid, should

bear the King of Glo - ry, in low - li - ness ar - ray'd. 2. Say, dore.

Additional Lyrics

2. Say, Mary, of salvation, who brought these tidings nigh,
This news of exaltation, whence comes it us anigh?
The angel Gabriel spake us, on entering this house,
That God shall not forsake us, but ransom, by His cross.

3. Believest thou the angel, O Mary, tell us true,
What answer gav'st thou Gabriel of joy for that ye knew?
The Lord of heav'n be praised both now and evermore,
Let songs of joy be raised, come hither and adore.

Coventry Carol

Words by Robert Croo
Traditional English Melody

Strum Pattern: 7, 9
Pick Pattern: 7, 9

1. Lul - lay, thou lit - tle ti - ny child. By, by, lul -
2., 3., 4. *See additional lyrics*

ly, lul - lay. _____ Lul - lay, thou lit - tle ti - ny

child. By, by, lul - ly, lul - lay. _____ lay! _____

Additional Lyrics

2. Oh, sisters too,
How may we do,
For to preserve this day?
This poor youngling,
For whom we sing
By, by, lully, lullay.

3. Herod the king,
In his raging,
Charged he hath this day.
His men of might,
In his own sight,
All young children to slay.

4. That woe is me,
Poor child for thee!
And ever morn and day,
For thy parting
Neither say nor sing
By, by, lully, lullay!

Glad Christmas Bells

Traditional American Carol

Strum Pattern: 9
Pick Pattern: 7

Joyfully

Glad ___ Christ - mas bells your ___ mu - sic tells the ___ sweet and pleas - ant

sto - ry, how ___ came to earth in ___ low - ly birth, the ___ Lord of life and glo - ry.

Deck the Hall

Traditional Welsh Carol

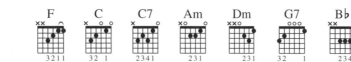

Strum Pattern: 4, 2
Pick Pattern: 4, 5

Verse
Gaily

Additional Lyrics

2. See the blazing yule before us;
   Fa, la, la, la, la, la, la, la, la.
   Strike the harp and join the chorus;
   Fa, la, la, la, la, la, la, la, la.
   Follow me in merry measure;
   Fa, la, la, la, la, la, la, la, la, la.
   While I tell of Yuletide treasure;
   Fa, la, la, la, la, la, la, la, la.

3. Fast away the old year passes;
   Fa, la, la, la, la, la, la, la, la.
   Hail the new ye lads and lasses;
   Fa, la, la, la, la, la, la, la, la.
   Sing we joyous, all together;
   Fa, la, la, la, la, la, la, la, la.
   Heedless of the wind and weather;
   Fa, la, la, la, la, la, la, la, la.

Ding Dong! Merrily on High!

French Carol

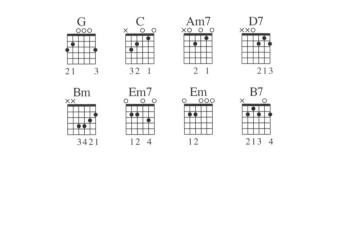

Strum Pattern: 4
Pick Pattern: 4

Verse
Moderately

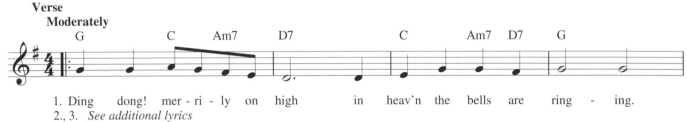

1. Ding dong! mer - ri - ly on high in heav'n the bells are ring - ing.
2., 3. *See additional lyrics*

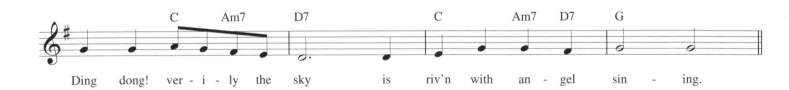

Ding dong! ver - i - ly the sky is riv'n with an - gel sing - ing.

Chorus

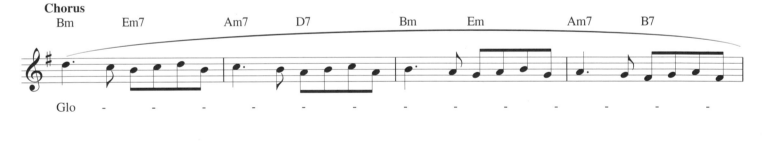

Glo - - - - - - - - - - -

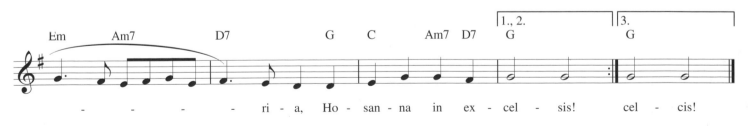

- - - - - ri - a, Ho - san - na in ex - cel - sis! cel - cis!

Additional Lyrics

2. E'en so here below, below, let steeple bells be swinging,
   And i-o, i-o, i-o, by priest and people singing.

3. Pray you, dutifully prime your matin chime, ye ringers;
   May you beautiful rime your evetime song, ye singers.

A Fire Is Started in Bethlehem

Traditional Castilian Carol

Strum Pattern: 3
Pick Pattern: 3

Verse
Moderately

1. Here in Beth - le - hem this eve - ning, springs a might - y flame from heav - en, whom our
2., 3. *See additional lyrics*

self - ish - ness will be con - sum - ing, and through whom we are for - giv - en.

Chorus

Flash - ing and splash - ing, the fish - es in the riv - er, splash - ing and bow - ing to

Christ from heav - en com - ing. Flash - ing and splash - ing, the fish - es in the wa - ter,

splash - ing and prais - ing the light from heav - en dawn - ing. 2. In a light from heav - en dawn - ing.

*Combine patterns 7 and 10

Additional Lyrics

2. In a cold and humble stable,
Blooms a perfect white carnation,
That becomes a lovely purple lily,
Sacrificed for our redemption.

3. Washing swaddling clothes for Jesus,
Mary by a stream is singing.
Sparrows chirp to hear a joyful greeting,
And the rippling brook is laughing.

The First Noël

17th Century English Carol
Music from W. Sandys' Christmas Carols

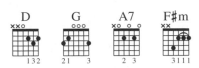

Strum Pattern: 7, 9
Pick Pattern: 7, 9

Additional Lyrics

2. They looked up and saw a star
   Shining in the east, beyond them far.
   And to the earth it gave great light
   And so it continued both day and night.

3. And by the light of that same star,
   Three wise man came from country far;
   To seek for a King was their intent,
   And to follow the star wherever it went.

4. This star drew nigh to the northwest,
   O'er Bethlehem it took its rest;
   And there it did both stop and stay,
   Right over the place where Jesus lay.

5. Then entered in those wise men three,
   Full reverently upon their knee;
   And offered there in His presence,
   Their gold, and myrrh, and frankincense.

The Friendly Beasts

Traditional English Carol

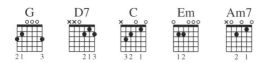

Strum Pattern: 7, 8
Pick Pattern: 8, 9

Verse

Moderately

1. Je - sus our broth - er, kind and good, was hum - bly
2.-6. *See additional lyrics*

born in a sta - ble rude; and the friend - ly beasts a - round Him

stood, Je - sus our broth - er kind and good. el.

Additional Lyrics

2. "I," said the donkey, shaggy and brown,
   "I carried his mother up hill and down.
   I carried his mother to Bethlehem town."
   "I," said the donkey, shaggy and brown.

3. "I," said the cow, all white and red,
   "I gave Him my manger for His bed.
   I gave Him my hay to pillow His head."
   "I," said the cow, all white and red.

4. "I," said the sheep with the curly horn,
   "I gave Him my wool for His blanket warm.
   He wore my coat on Christmas morn."
   "I," said the sheep with the curly horn.

5. "I," said the dove from the rafters high,
   "I cooed Him to sleep that He would not cry.
   We cooed Him to sleep, my mate and I."
   "I," said the dove from the rafters high.

6. Thus every beast by some good spell,
   In the stable dark was glad to tell
   Of the gift he gave Emmanuel,
   The gift he gave Emmanuel.

From Out the Deep Woods a Cuckoo Flew

Traditional Czech Carol

Strum Pattern: 7
Pick Pattern: 7

Verse
Moderately

1. From out the deep woods a cuck - oo flew, cuck - oo!
2. *See additional lyrics*

Seek - ing the heav - en - ly Babe to woo, cuck - oo! Near

Je - sus' bed, he gave___ in songs the praise that to our

God___ be - longs, cuck - oo, cuck - oo, cuck - oo! roo!

Additional Lyrics

2. High in the rafters there sat a dove, cooroo!
Cooing to Jesus of his great love, cooroo!
His heart and voice so full of joy
That heaven sent this lovely Boy!
Cooroo, cooroo, cooroo!

From the Eastern Mountains

Traditional

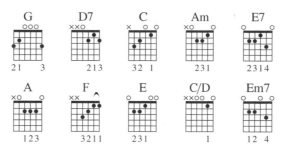

Strum Pattern: 4
Pick Pattern: 1

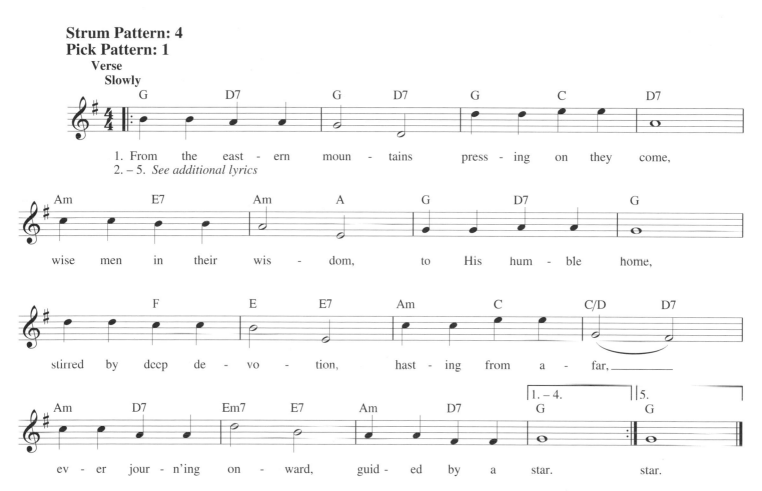

1. From the east-ern moun-tains press-ing on they come,
2. – 5. *See additional lyrics*

wise men in their wis - dom, to His hum - ble home,

stirred by deep de - vo - tion, hast - ing from a - far,_____

ev - er jour - n'ing on - ward, guid - ed by a star. star.

Additional Lyrics

2. There their Lord and Savior
   Meek and lowly lay,
   Wondrous light that led them
   Onward on their way,
   Ever now to lighten
   Nations from afar,
   As they journey homeward
   By that guiding star.

3. Thou who in a manger
   Once hast lowly lain,
   Who dost now in glory
   O'er all kingdoms reign,
   Gather in the heathen
   Who in lands afar
   Ne'er have seen the brightness
   Of Thy guiding star.

4. Gather in the outcasts,
   All who have astray,
   Throw Thy radiance o'er them,
   Guide them on their way,
   Those who never knew Thee,
   Those who have wandered far,
   Guide them by the brightness
   Of Thy guiding star.

5. Onward through the darkness
   Of the lonely night,
   Shining still before them
   With Thy kindly light,
   Guide them, Jew and Gentile,
   Homeward from afar,
   Young and old together,
   By Thy guiding star.

Fum, Fum, Fum

Traditional Catalonian Carol

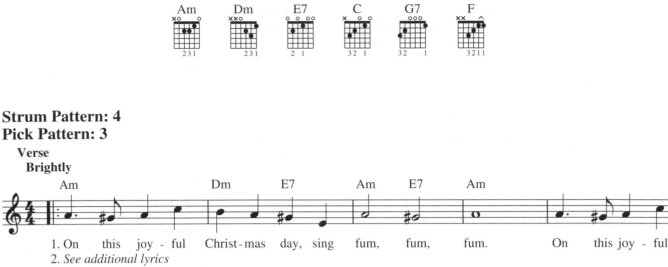

Strum Pattern: 4
Pick Pattern: 3

Verse
Brightly

1. On this joy-ful Christ-mas day, sing fum, fum, fum. On this joy-ful
2. *See additional lyrics*

Christ-mas day, sing fum, fum, fum. For a bless-ed Babe was

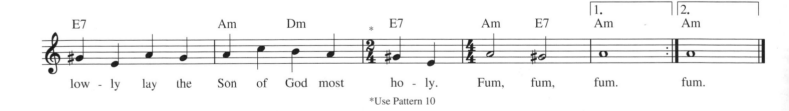

born up-on this day at break of morn. In a man-ger poor and

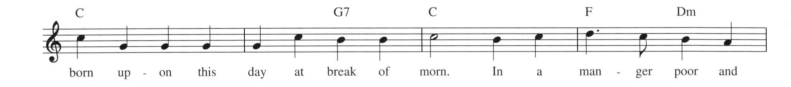

low-ly lay the Son of God most ho-ly. Fum, fum, fum. fum.

*Use Pattern 10

Additional Lyrics

2. Thanks to God for holidays, sing fum, fum, fum.
Thanks to God for holidays, sing fum, fum, fum.
Now we all our voices raise.
And sing a song of grateful praise.
Celebrate in song and story, all the wonders of His glory.
Fum, fum, fum.

Gather Around the Christmas Tree

By John H. Hopkins

G D7 B7 Em Am D A7sus4 A7 C

Strum Pattern: 4
Pick Pattern: 5

Verse
Lively

1. Gath - er a-round the Christ - mas tree! Gath - er a-round the Christ - mas tree!
2., 3. *See additional lyrics*

Ev - er green have its branch - es been, it is king of all the wood - land scene. For

Christ, our King is born to - day, His reign shall nev - er pass a - way. Ho -

Chorus

| 1., 2. | 3. |

san - na, Ho - san - na, Ho - san - na in the high - est! high - est!

Additional Lyrics

2. Gather around the Christmas tree!
   Gather around the Christmas tree!
   Once the pride of the mountainside,
   Now cut down to grace our Christmastide.
   For Christ from heav'n to earth came down
   To gain, through death, a nobler crown.

3. Gather around the Christmas tree!
   Gather around the Christmas tree!
   Ev'ry bough has a burden now,
   They are gifts of love for us, we trow.
   For Christ is born, His love to show
   And give good gifts to men below.

Go, Tell It on the Mountain

African-American Spiritual
Verses by John W. Work, Jr.

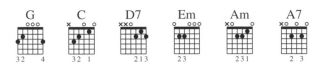

Strum Pattern: 2, 3
Pick Pattern: 3, 4

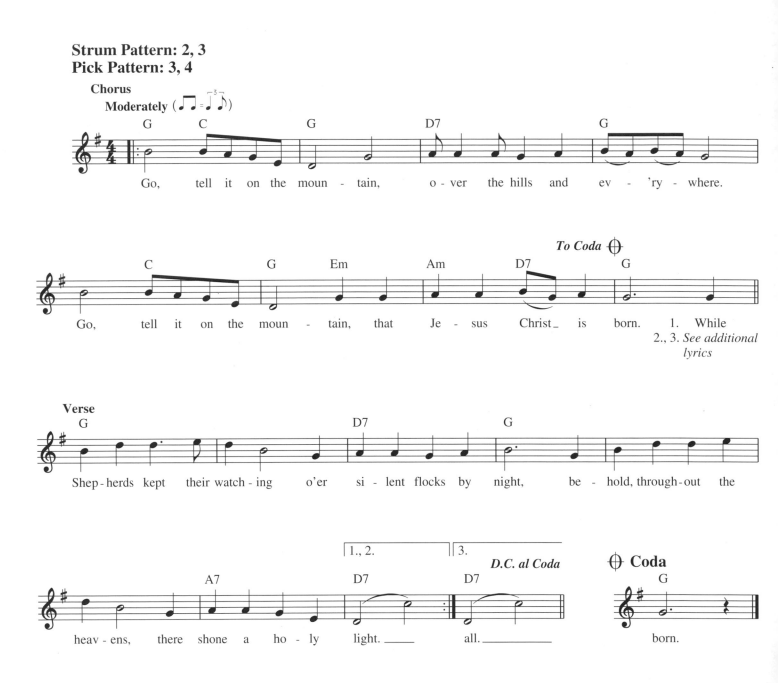

Additional Lyrics

2. The shepherds feared and trembled
   When, lo! above the earth
   Rang out the angel chorus
   That hailed our Savior's birth.

3. Down in a lowly manger
   Our humble Christ was born,
   And God sent us salvation
   That blessed Christmas morn.

God Rest Ye Merry, Gentlemen

19th Century English Carol

Strum Pattern: 3, 5
Pick Pattern: 3, 4

Additional Lyrics

2. In Bethlehem, in Jewry
    This blessed babe was born
    And laid within a manger
    Upon this blessed morn
    To which His mother Mary
    Did nothing take in scorn.

3. From God, our Heav'nly Father,
    A blessed angel came,
    And unto certain shepherds
    Brought tidings of the same.
    How that in Bethlehem was born.
    The Son of God by name.

Going to Bethlehem

Traditional Chilean Carol

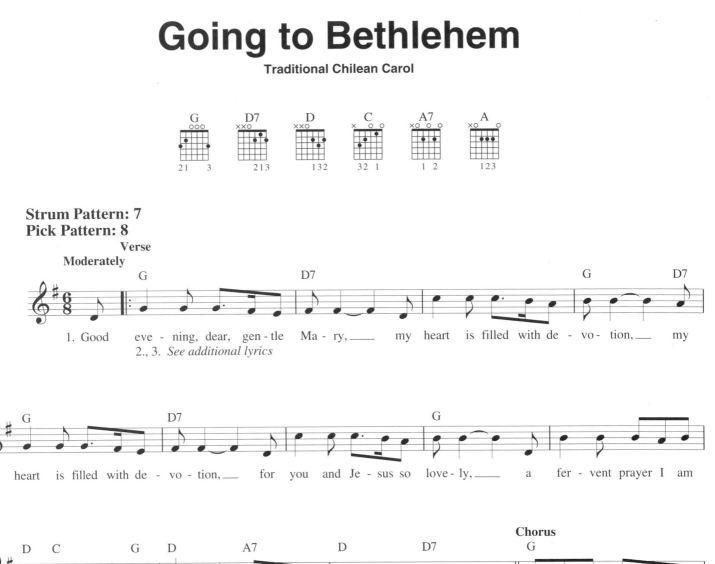

Strum Pattern: 7
Pick Pattern: 8

Verse
Moderately

1. Good eve - ning, dear, gen - tle Ma - ry, ___ my heart is filled with de - vo - tion, ___ my
2., 3. *See additional lyrics*

heart is filled with de - vo - tion, ___ for you and Je - sus so love - ly, ___ a fer - vent prayer I am

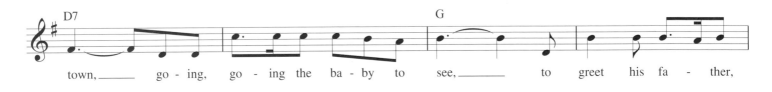

Chorus

off - 'ring, ___ a fer - vent prayer I am off - 'ring. Go - ing, go - ing, to Beth - le - hem

town, ___ go - ing, go - ing the ba - by to see, ___ to greet his fa - ther,

Jo - seph, ___ and Ma - ry, on bend - ed knee. 2. Good Ma - ry, on bend - ed knee.

Additional Lyrics

2. Goodbye to you little Manuel,
   Until the New Year beginning,
   Until the New Year beginning,
   I'll see you after the shearing,
   So rich from wool you'll be selling,
   So rich from wool you'll be selling.

3. O Mary, holiest Mother,
   As pure as flowers unfolding,
   As pure as flowers unfolding,
   I come on this eve of Christmas,
   Thy love and glory beholding,
   Thy love and glory beholding.

The Golden Carol

Old English Carol

Strum Pattern: 8
Pick Pattern: 8

Verse
Moderately

1. We saw a light shine out a-far, on Christ-mas in the morn-ing, and
2. *See additional lyrics*

straight we knew it was Christ's star, bright beam-ing in the morn-ing. Then

did we fall on bend-ed knee, on Christ-mas in the morn-ing, and

prais'd the Lord, who'd let us see His glo-ry at its dawn-ing. 2. Oh! morn-ing.

Additional Lyrics

2. Oh! Ever thought be of His name,
   On Christmas in the morning,
   Who bore for us both grief and shame,
   Afflictions sharpest scorning.
   And may we die (when death shall come),
   On Christmas in the morning,
   And see in heav'n, our glori'us home,
   That star of Christmas morning.

Good Christian Men, Rejoice

14th Century Latin Text

Translated by John Mason Neale

14th Century German Melody

Strum Pattern: 9

Pick Pattern: 7

Additional Lyrics

2. Good Christian men, rejoice
With heart and soul and voice.
Now ye hear of endless bliss: Joy! Joy!
Jesus Christ was born for this!
He hath op'd the heavenly door,
And man is blessed evermore.
Christ was born for this!
Christ was born for this!

3. Good Christian men, rejoice
With heart and soul and voice.
Now ye need not fear the grave: Peace! Peace!
Jesus Christ was born to save!
Calls you one and calls you all,
To gain His everlasting hall.
Christ was born to save!
Christ was born to save!

Good King Wenceslas

Words by John M. Neale
Music from Piae Cantiones

Strum Pattern: 4, 3
Pick Pattern: 5, 3

Verse

With spirit

1. Good King Wen - ces - las looked out on the feast of Ste - phen;
2.-5. *See additional lyrics*

when the snow lay 'round a - bout, deep and crisp and e - ven.

Bright - ly shone the moon that night, though the frost was cru - el; when a poor man

came in sight, gath - 'ring win - ter fu - el. ing.

Additional Lyrics

2. "Hither page, and stand by me,
If thou know'st it, telling;
Yonder peasant, who is he?
Where and what his dwelling?"
"Sire, he lives a good league hence,
Underneath the mountain;
Right against the forest fence,
By Saint Agnes' fountain."

3. "Bring me flesh, and bring me wine,
Bring me pine-logs hither;
Thou and I will see him dine,
When we bear them thither."
Page and monarch forth they went,
Forth they went together;
Through the rude winds wild lament,
And the bitter weather.

4. "Sire, the night is darker now,
And the wind blows stronger;
Fails my heart, I know not how,
I can go not longer."
"Mark my footsteps, my good page,
Tread thou in them boldly:
Thou shalt find the winter's rage
Freeze thy blood less coldly."

5. In his master's steps he trod,
Where the snow lay dinted;
Heat was in the very sod
Which the saint has printed.
Therefore, Christian men, be sure,
Wealth or rank possessing;
Ye who now will bless the poor,
Shall yourselves find blessing.

The Happy Christmas Comes Once More

Words by Nicolai F.S. Grundtvig
Music by C. Balle

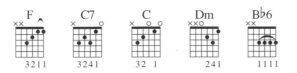

Strum Pattern: 7
Pick Pattern: 7

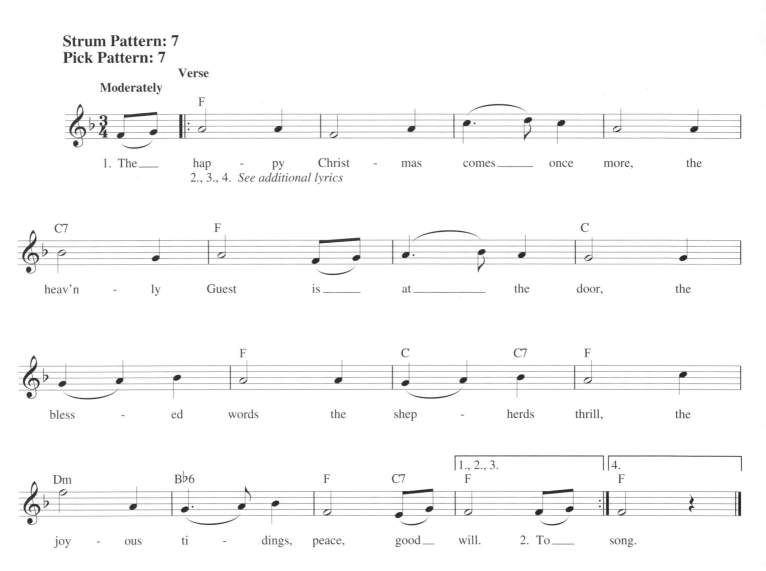

Additional Lyrics

2. To David's city let us fly,
   Where angels sing beneath the sky,
   Through plain and village pressing near,
   And news from God with shepherds hear.

3. O, let us go with quiet mind,
   The gentle Babe with shepherds find,
   To gaze on Him who gladdens them,
   The loveliest flow'r on Jesse's stem.

4. Come, Jesus glorious heav'nly guest,
   Keep Thine own Christmas in our breast;
   Then David's harp-string, hushed so long
   Shall swell our jubilee of song.

Hark! The Herald Angels Sing

Words by Charles Wesley
Altered by George Whitefield
Music by Felix Mendelssohn-Bartholdy
Arranged by William H. Cummings

Strum Pattern: 2, 3
Pick Pattern: 3, 4

Additional Lyrics

2. Christ, by highest heav'n adored,
   Christ, the everlasting Lord;
   Late in time behold Him come,
   Offspring of the Virgin's womb.
   Veil'd in flesh the Godhead see:
   Hail th'Incarnate Deity.
   Pleased as Man with man to dwell,
   Jesus, our Emmanuel!
   Hark! The hearld angels sing,
   "Glory to the newborn King."

3. Mild, He lays His glory by,
   Born that man no more may die;
   Born to raise the sons of earth,
   Born to give them second birth.
   Ris'n with healing in His wings,
   Light and life to all He brings.
   Hail the Son of Righteousness!
   Hail, the heav'n-born Prince of Peace!
   Hark! The hearld angels sing,
   "Glory to the newborn King."

He Is Born

Traditional French Carol

Strum Pattern: 10
Pick Pattern: 10

Additional Lyrics

2. Oh, how lovely, oh, how pure,
Is this perfect child of heaven.
Oh, how lovely, oh, how pure,
Gracious gift of God to man.

3. Jesus, Lord of all the world,
Coming as a child among us,
Jesus, Lord of all the world,
Grant to us Thy heav'nly peace.

Hear Them Bells

Words and Music by D.S. McCosh

Strum Pattern: 3
Pick Pattern: 3

Verse
Brightly

Hear them bells, ____ mer - ry Christ - mas bells! ____ They are ring - ing out the

e - vil of the sword. ____ Hear them bells, ____ mer - ry Christ - mas bells! ____

They are ring - ing in the glo - ry of the Lord! ____

Hear, O Shepherds

Traditional Croation Carol

Strum Pattern: 3
Pick Pattern: 3

Moderately

Hear, O shep - herds, hear while I tell you, hark to the mir - a - cle that

on - ly now be - fell you. On a man - ger low - ly, in a prick - ly stall

lies the Ba - by ho - ly who will save us all, lies the Ba - by ho - ly who will save us all.

The Holly and the Ivy

18th Century English Carol

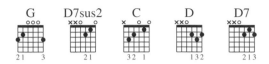

Strum Pattern: 8
Pick Pattern: 8

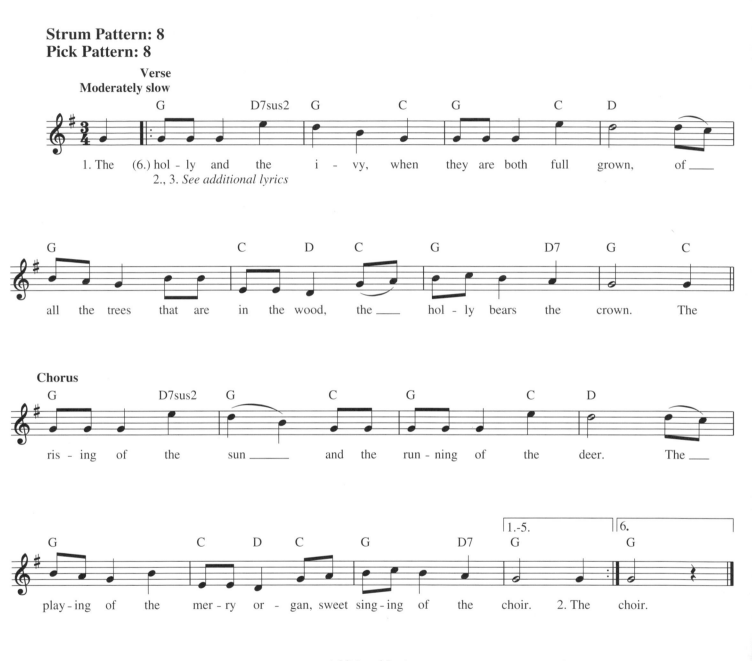

Additional Lyrics

2. The holly bears a blossom,
   As white as lily flow'r,
   And Mary bore sweet Jesus Christ,
   To be our sweet Saviour.

3. The holly bears a berry,
   As red as any blood,
   And Mary bore sweet Jesus Christ,
   To do poor sinners good.

4. The holly bears a pickle,
   As sharp as any thorn,
   And Mary bore sweet Jesus Christ
   On Christmas Day in the morn.

5. The holly bears a bark,
   As bitter as any gall,
   And Mary bore sweet Jesus Christ
   For to redeem us all.

How Brightly Beams the Morning Star

Words and Music by Philipp Nicolai
Translated by William Mercer
Harmonized by J.S. Bach

Strum Pattern: 4
Pick Pattern: 3

Additional Lyrics

2. The ray of God that breaks our night.
   And fills the darkened souls with light,
   Who long for truth were pining.

3. Through Thee alone can we be blest;
   Then deep be on our hearts imprest
   The love that thou hast borne us.

4. So make us ready to fulfill
   With burning zeal Thy holy will,
   Though men may vex or scorn us.

Chorus 2. Saviour, let us never lose Thee,
   For we choose Thee,
   Thirst to know Thee
   All we are and have we owe Thee!

5. O praise to Him who came to save,
   Who conquer'd death and burst the grave.
   Each day new praise resoundeth.

6. To Him the Lamb who once was slain,
   The Friend whom none shall trust in vain,
   Whose grace for ay aboundeth.

Chorus 3. Sing, ye heavens, tell the story
   Of His glory,
   Till His praises
   Flood with light earth's darkest places!

I Am So Glad on Christmas Eve

Words by Marie Wexelsen
Music by Peder Knudsen

Strum Pattern: 7
Pick Pattern: 8

Verse
Moderately

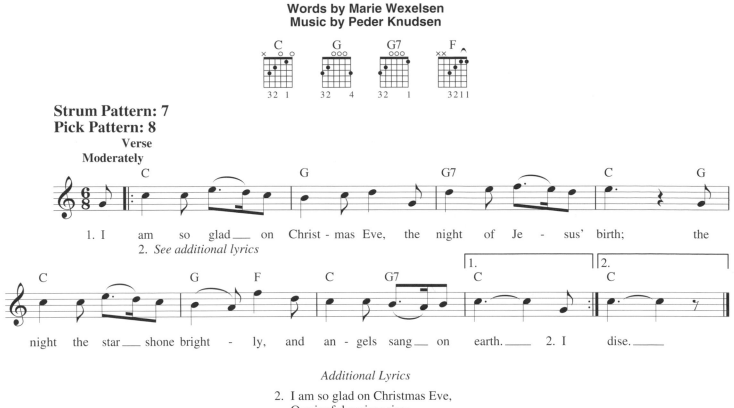

1. I am so glad on Christ-mas Eve, the night of Je-sus' birth; the
2. *See additional lyrics*

night the star shone bright-ly, and an-gels sang on earth. 2. I dise.

Additional Lyrics

2. I am so glad on Christmas Eve,
   Our joyful praises rise;
   To Jesus, who has opened wide,
   His own sweet paradise.

I Heard the Bells on Christmas Day

Words by Henry Wadsworth Longfellow
Music by John Baptiste Calkin

Strum Pattern: 4
Pick Pattern: 3

Verse
Moderately slow

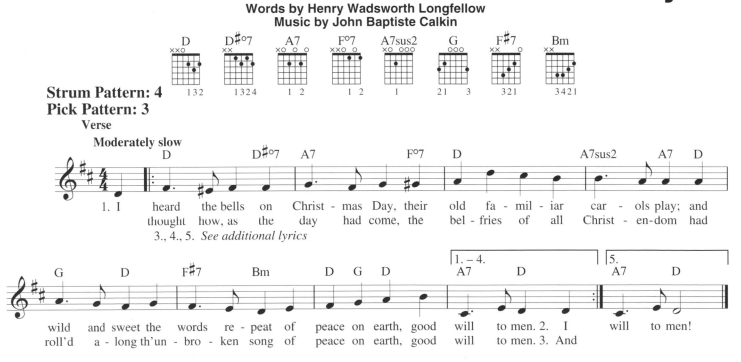

1. I heard the bells on Christ-mas Day, their old fa-mil-iar car-ols play; and
   thought how, as the day had come, the bel-fries of all Christ-en-dom had
3., 4., 5. *See additional lyrics*

wild and sweet the words re-peat of peace on earth, good will to men. 2. I will to men!
roll'd a-long th'un-bro-ken song of peace on earth, good will to men. 3. And

Additional Lyrics

3. And in despair I bow'd my head:
   "There is no peace on earth," I said.
   "For hate is strong, and mocks the song
   Of peace on earth, good will to men."

4. Then pealed the bells more loud and deep:
   "God is not dead, nor doth He sleep;
   The wrong shall fail, the right prevail,
   With peace on earth, good will to men."

5. Till, ringing, singing on its way,
   The world revolved from night to day,
   A voice, a chime, a chant sublime,
   Of peace on earth, good will to men!

I Go to Bethlehem

Traditional Czech Carol

Strum Pattern: 9
Pick Pattern: 7

Verse
Moderately

1. I go to Beth-le-hem, to see the
2. *See additional lyrics*

ti-ny child. My black roos-ter, trim and sleek, my cuck-oo with

song so sweet: These will I give Him. give Him.

Chorus

Coo, coo-coo! Coo, coo-coo! Je-sus, He sings for you!

Coo, coo-coo! Coo, coo-coo! Je-sus, He sings for you!

Additional Lyrics

2. Rooster will crow away
   Making the Baby gay.
   Cuckoo perching near His little head,
   Calling softly will make His heart glad:
   These will I give Him.

I Saw Three Ships

Traditional English Carol

Strum Pattern: 8, 7
Pick Pattern: 8, 9

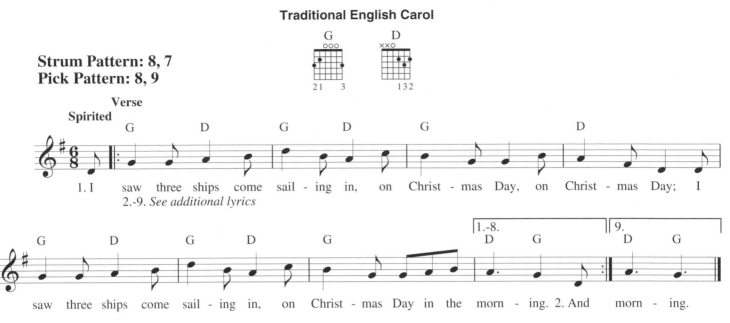

1. I saw three ships come sail-ing in, on Christ-mas Day, on Christ-mas Day; I

2.-9. *See additional lyrics*

saw three ships come sail-ing in, on Christ-mas Day in the morn - ing. 2. And morn - ing.

Addiotnal Lyrics

2. And what was in those ships, all three?
3. Our Savior Christ and His lady.
4. Pray, whither sailed those ships all three?
5. O, they sailed into Bethlehem.
6. And all the bells on earth shall ring.
7. And all the angels in heaven shall sing.
8. And all the souls on earth shall sing.
9. Then let us all rejoice amain!

Love Came Down at Christmas

Text by Christina Rossetti
Traditional Irish Melody

Strum Pattern: 4
Pick Pattern: 4

1. Love came down at Christ - mas, love all love - ly, love di - vine,

2., 3. *See additional lyrics*

love was born at Christ - mas, star and an - gels gave the sign. gift and sign.

Additional Lyrics

2. Worship we the God head,
   Love incarnate, love divine,
   Worship we our Jesus,
   But wherewith for sacred sign?

3. Love shall be our token,
   Love be yours and love be mine,
   Love to God and neighbor,
   Love for plea and gift and sign.

In Bethlehem's Cradle

Traditional Puerto Rican Carol

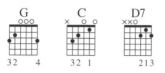

Strum Pattern: 7
Pick Pattern: 7

1. He is born with-in a sta-ble, in the bit-ter cold of win-ter, 'twixt the
2., 3., 4. *See additional lyrics*

ox and ass He's ly-ing, Heav-en's Child, the world's re-deem-er. Sing now of

Chorus

Je-sus, of the dear Ba-by, O what a glo-rious gift from a-bove! He has our

hearts and all of our love! He has our hearts and all of our love! Le-rum,

le-rum, le-rum, la! ¡Que vi-va! 2. There with- ¡Que vi-va!

Additional Lyrics

2. There within the dingy stable,
   Sun and moon and star are shining,
   Joseph, Mary and the Child,
   For whom all our hearts were pining.

3. To His side, a lowly shepherd,
   From the Spanish fields appearing,
   Brings the Baby gifts of linen,
   So a shirt He can be wearing.

4. Also near Him stands a gypsy,
   From Granada he comes hieing,
   Bringing to the Child a rooster,
   "Cock-a-doodle-doo," it's crying.

Infant Holy, Infant Lowly

Traditonal Polish Carol

Strum Pattern: 7, 9
Pick Pattern: 7, 9

Verse

Lyrically

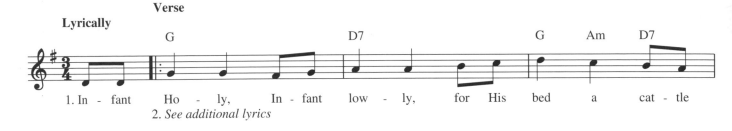

1. In - fant Ho - ly, In - fant low - ly, for His bed a cat - tle
2. *See additional lyrics*

stall. Ox - en low - ing, lit - tle know - ing Christ the Babe is Lord of

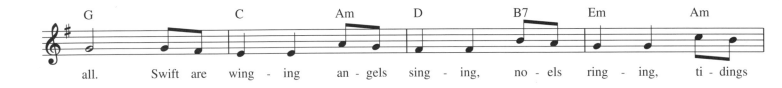

all. Swift are wing - ing an - gels sing - ing, no - els ring - ing, ti - dings

bring - ing: Christ the Babe is Lord of all! 2. Flocks are you.

Additional Lyrics

2. Flocks are sleeping, shepherds keeping
    Vigil 'til the morning new.
    Saw the glory, heard the story,
    Tidings of a Gospel true.
    Thus rejoicing, free from sorrow,
    Praises voicing, greet the morrow:
    Christ the Babe was born for you.

Infant So Gentle

Traditional French Carol

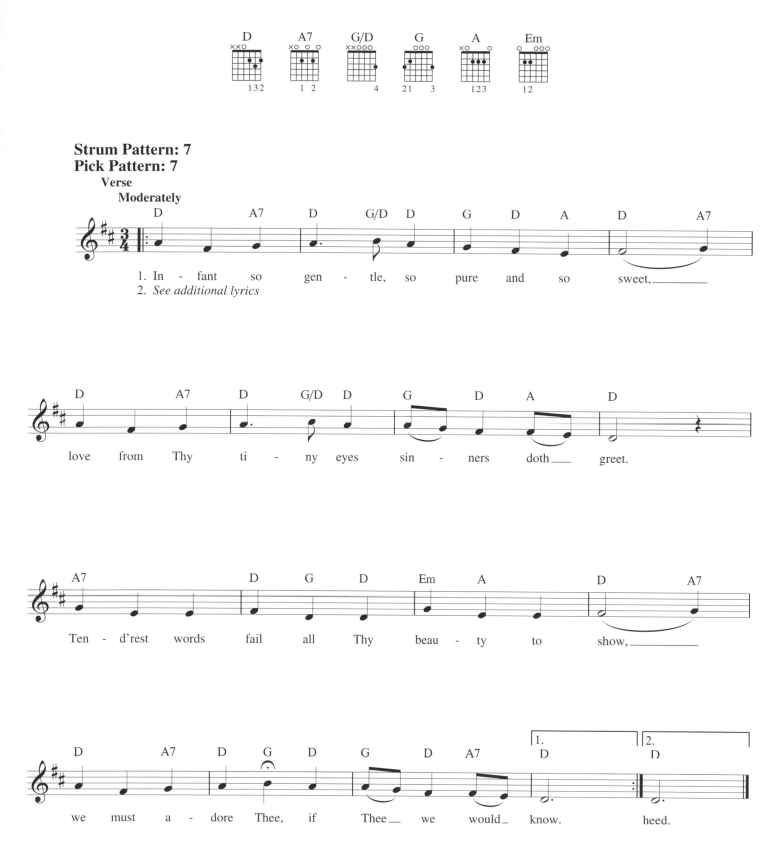

Additional Lyrics

2. Infant so holy, so meek and so mild,
   We come to welcome Thee, our dear Christ Child.
   We cannot tell Thee how much we do need
   Thy precious presence, all sinners take heed.

Irish Carol

Traditional Irish Carol

*Strum Pattern: 8
*Pick Pattern: 8

Verse
Moderately

*Play pattern 2x per measure.

Additional Lyrics

2. But why should we rejoice, should we not rather mourn,
   To see the hope of nations thus in a stable born?
   Where there no sumptuous palace, nor any inn at all,
   To lodge His heav'nly mother, but in a filthy stall?

3. Oh cease, ye blessed angels, such clam'rous joys to make!
   Though midnight silence favours, the shepherds are awake.
   And somewhere else your lustre, your rags elsewhere display,
   For Herod may slay the Babe, and Christ must straight away.

4. If we would then rejoice, let's cancel the old score,
   And purposing amendment, resolve to sin no more.
   For dancing, sporting, rev'ling with masquerade and drum,
   So Christmas merry be, as Christians doth become.

It Came Upon the Midnight Clear

Words by Edmund H. Sears
Traditional English Melody
Adapted by Arthur Sullivan

Strum Pattern: 8, 7
Pick Pattern: 8, 9

Jesus, the Newborn Baby

Traditional Italian Carol

Strum Pattern: 3, 4
Pick Pattern: 4, 5

Verse
Moderately

1. Je - sus, the new - born Ba - by, lies here in Beth - le -
2. *See additional lyrics*

hem; born in a hum - ble man - ger, is heav - en's pre - cious

Gem. He is a pre - cious Gem, al - though we find Him cry - ing! In Ma - ry's arms He's

sigh - ing, Je - sus, our Di - a - dem. Son!

Additional Lyrics

2. We hear a gentle voice sing
Songs for the Holy One,
Joseph, the Baby's father,
Nestles Him close and warm.
"Sleep sweetly my dear Son."
O see him comfort Jesus,
His tiny Baby soothing!
Glory to God's own Son!

Jingle Bells

Words and Music by J. Pierpont

Strum Pattern: 2, 3
Pick Pattern: 3, 4

Verse
Brightly

1. Dash-ing through the snow, in a one horse o-pen sleigh. O'er the fields we go,
2., 3. *See additional lyrics*

laugh-ing all the way. Bells on bob-tail ring, mak-ing spir-its bright. What fun it is to

ride and sing a sleigh-ing song to - night! Oh! Jin - gle bells, jin - gle bells, jin - gle all the

Chorus

way. Oh, what fun it is to ride in a one horse o - pen sleigh! ___ Jin - gle bells,

jin - gle bells, jin - gle all the way. Oh, what fun it is to ride in a one horse o-pen sleigh! 2. A sleigh!

Additional Lyrics

2. A day or two ago, I thought I'd take a ride,
   And soon Miss Fannie Bright was sitting by my side.
   The horse was lean and lank,
   Misfortune seemed his lot.
   He got into a drifted bank and we, we got upshot! Oh!

3. Now the ground is white, go it while you're young.
   Take the girls tonight and sing this sleighing song.
   Just get a bobtail bay,
   Two-forty for his speed.
   Then hitch him to an open sleigh and
   Crack, you'll take the lead! Oh!

Jolly Old St. Nicholas

Traditional 19th Century American Carol

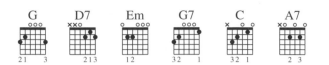

Strum Pattern: 10
Pick Pattern: 10

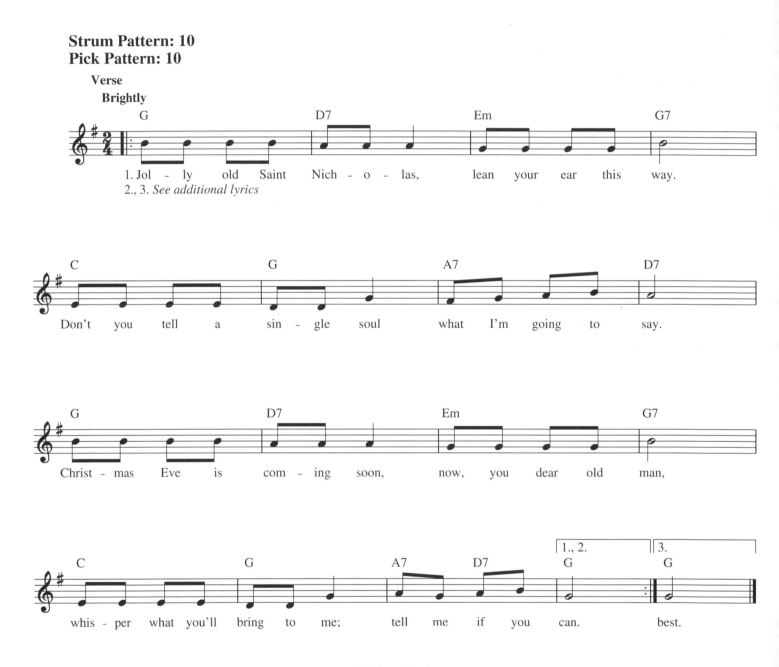

Additional Lyrics

2. When the clock is striking twelve, when I'm fast asleep.
   Down the chimney broad and black, with your pack you'll creep.
   All the stockings you will find hanging in a row.
   Mine will be the shortest one, you'll be sure to know.

3. Johnny wants a pair of skates; Susy wants a sled.
   Nellie wants a picture book, yellow, blue and red.
   Now I think I'll leave to you what to give the rest.
   Choose for me, dear Santa Claus.
   You will know the best.

Joseph Dearest, Joseph Mine

Traditional German Carol

Strum Pattern: 7
Pick Pattern: 7

Verse
Moderately

1. Jo - seph, dear - est Jo - seph mine, help me cra - dle the Babe di - vine,
2. *See additional lyrics*

sing to Him a lull - a - bye: "Now sleep and rest, Your slum - ber blest, O

Chorus

Je - sus!" He came a - mong us at Christ - mas time, at Christ - mas time in

Beth - le - hem, bring - ing all men far and wide love's di - a - dem. Ei - a,

ei - a. Je - sus Christ, who came to earth to save us. save us.

Additional Lyrics

2. Gladly, Mother Mary mine,
   Will I rock the Babe divine,
   While I sing a lullabye:
   "O sleep and rest, Your slumber blest, O Jesus."

Joy to the World

Words by Isaac Watts
Music by George Frideric Handel
Arranged by Lowell Mason

Strum Pattern: 3
Pick Pattern: 3

Verse
With spirit

1. Joy to the World! The Lord is come: Let earth re-
2., 3., 4. *See additional lyrics*

ceive her King. Let ev - 'ry heart pre - pare Him

room, and heav - en and na - ture sing, and heav - en and na - ture

sing, and heav - en and heav - en and na - ture sing. love.

Additional Lyrics

2. Joy to the world! The Savior reigns;
   Let men their songs employ;
   While fields and floods,
   Rocks, hills and plains,
   Repeat the sounding joy,
   Repeat the sounding joy,
   Repeat, repeat the sounding joy.

3. No more let sin and sorrow grow,
   Nor thorns infest the ground;
   He comes to make His blessings flow
   Far as the curse is found,
   Far as the curse is found,
   Far as, far as the curse is found.

4. He rules the world with truth and grace
   And makes the nations prove
   The glories of His righteousness,
   And wonders of His love,
   And wonders of His love,
   And wonders, wonders of His love.

Let Our Gladness Know No End

Traditional Bohemian Carol

Additional Lyrics

2. See the lovel'est blooming rose, hallelujah!
From the branch of Jesse grows, hallelujah.

3. Into flesh is made the word, hallelujah!
'Tis our refuge, Christ the Lord, hallelujah.

Lullaby, Jesus

Traditional Polish Carol

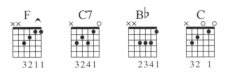

Strum Pattern: 7
Pick Pattern: 7

Verse
Moderately

1. Lull - a - by, Je - sus, O cease from your cry - ing,
2. *See additional lyrics*

here on Thy Moth - er's warm breast sweet - ly ly - ing.

Chorus

Lull - a - by, Je - sus, O sleep now, my pre - cious,

Moth - er is watch - ing with love none can meas - ure. meas - ure.

Additional Lyrics

2. See how God's earth
   Lies in sorrow and sadness;
   Give us Thy blessing,
   O bring heaven's gladness!

March of the Three Kings

Words by M.L. Hohman
Traditional French Melody

Strum Pattern: 10
Pick Pattern: 10

Mary Had a Baby

African-American Spiritual

Strum Pattern: 1, 3
Pick Pattern: 1, 3

Additional Lyrics

3. She called Him Jesus,
4. Where was He born?
5. Born in a stable,
6. Where did they lay Him?
7. Laid Him in a manger,

O Bethlehem

Traditional Spanish

Strum Pattern: 7
Pick Pattern: 7

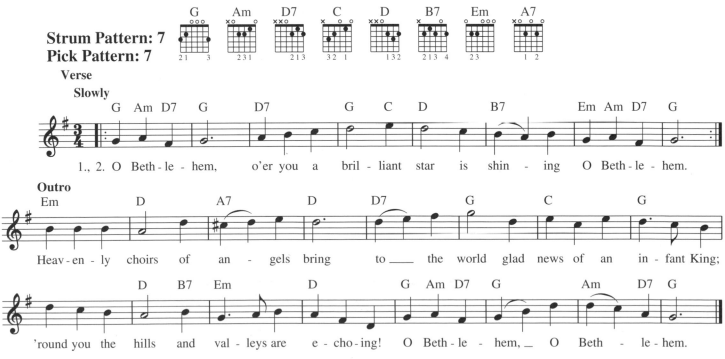

Mary, Dear Mother of Jesus

Traditional Italian Carol

Strum Pattern: 7
Pick Pattern: 7

Verse
Moderately

1. Ma - ry, dear moth - er of Je - sus, our Lord, we
2. *See additional lyrics*

haste to the crib with joy - ful ac - cord,

to see God's own gift on this Christ - mas ___ Day, ___

voic - ing our prais - es, the ___ star lights our way. love.

Additional Lyrics

2. Mary, sweet mother of the Holy Child,
Born that all mankind might be reconciled,
Thy infant Son was God-sent from above,
All thanks be to Him, for this gift of love.

O Christmas Tree

Traditional German Carol

Strum Pattern: 8, 7
Pick Pattern: 8, 9

Additional Lyrics

2. O, Christmas tree! O, Christmas tree,
   Much pleasure doth thou bring me!
   O, Christmas tree! O, Christmas tree,
   Much pleasure does thou bring me!
   For every year the Christmas tree
   Brings to us all both joy and glee.
   O, Christmas tree, O, Christmas tree,
   Much pleasure doth thou bring me!

3. O, Christmas tree! O, Christmas tree,
   Thy candles shine out brightly!
   O, Christmas Tree, O, Christmas tree,
   Thy candles shine out brightly!
   Each bough doth hold its tiny light
   That makes each toy to sparkle bright.
   O, Christmas tree, O Christmas tree,
   Thy candles shine out brightly.

O Come, All Ye Faithful
(Adeste Fideles)

Words and Music by John Francis Wade
Latin Words translated by Frederick Oakeley

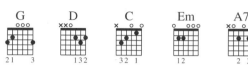

Strum Pattern: 4
Pick Pattern: 4, 5

Additional Lyrics

2. Sing choirs of angels, sing in exultation.
   O sing all ye citizens of heaven above.
   Glory to God in the highest.

3. Yea, Lord, we greet Thee, born this happy morning,
   Jesus, to Thee be all glory giv'n.
   Word of the Father, now in flesh appearing:

O Come, Little Children

Words by C. von Schmidt
Music J.P.A. Schulz

Strum Pattern: 10
Pick Pattern: 10

Verse
Quietly

1. O come, lit-tle chil-dren, from cot and from hall, O come to the
"Glo-ry to God!" sing the an-gels on high, and "Peace up-on

man-ger in Beth-le-hem's stall. There meek-ly He li-eth, the
earth!" heav'n-ly voic-es re-ply. Then come lit-tle chil-dren and

heav-en-ly child, so poor and so hum-ble, so sweet and so mild. 2. Now Day.
join in the day that glad-dened the world on that first Christ-mas

Pat-A-Pan
(Willie, Take Your Little Drum)

Words and Music by Bernard de la Monnoye

Strum Pattern: 2, 3
Pick Pattern: 2, 3

Verse
Very fast

1. Wil-lie, take your lit-tle drum. Ro-bin, bring your flute, and
men of old-en days gave the King of Kings their
man to-day be-come close-ly joined as flute and

come. Aren't they fun to play up-on? Tu-re-lu-re-lu, pat-a-pat-a-
praise, they had pipes to play up-on. Tu-re-lu-re-lu, pat-a-pat-a-
drum. Let the joy-ous tune play on! Tu-re-lu-re-lu, pat-a-pat-a-

pan. When you play your fife and drum, how can an-y-one be glum? 2. When the Day.
pan. And al-so the drums they'd play, full of joy on __ Christ-mas Day. 3. God and
pan. As the in-stru-ments you play, we will sing this __ Christ-mas

O Come, O Come Immanuel

Plainsong, 13th Century
Words translated by John M. Neale and Henry S. Coffin

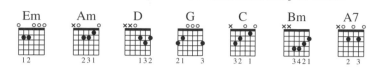

Strum Pattern: 4
Pick Pattern: 5

Verse
Slowly and expressively

1. O come, O come Im - man - u - el, and
2., 3. *See additional lyrics*

ran - som cap - tive Is - ra - el, that mourns in lone - ly

ex - ile here un - til the Son of God _____ ap -

Chorus

pear. Re - joice, re - joice! Im - man - u -

el shall come to thee, O Is - ra - el! 2. O el!

Additional Lyrics

2. O come Thou Wisdom from on high,
   And order all things far and nigh;
   To us the path of knowledge show,
   And cause us in her ways to go.

3. O come Desire of nations, bind
   All people in one heart and mind;
   Bid envy, strife, and quarrel's cease;
   Fill the whole world with heaven's peace.

O Holy Night

French Words by Placide Cappeau
English Words by John S. Dwight
Music by Adolphe Adam

Strum Pattern: 7, 9
Pick Pattern: 7, 9

Verse
Slowly and flowing

1. O Ho - ly night ____ the stars are bright - ly shin - ing, it is the
2. *See additional lyrics*

night of the dear Sav - ior's birth. ____ Long lay the world ____ in

sin and er - ror pin - ing, 'til He ap - peared and the soul felt its

worth. ____ A thrill of hope the wear - y soul re -

joic - es, for yon - der breaks a new and glor - ious morn.

Chorus

See additional lyrics

Fall _____ on your knees, _____ oh, hear _____ the an - gel voic - es! O night _____ di - vine, _____ O night _____ when Christ was born! _____ O night! _____ O

1.

Ho - ly night! O night di - vine! _____

2.

pow'r _____ and glo - ry _____

ev - er - more pro - claim. _____

Additional lyrics

2. Truly He taught us to love one another.
   His law is love, and His gospel is peace.
   Chains shall He break, for the slave is our brother,
   And in His name all oppression shall cease.
   Sweet hymns of joy in grateful chorus raise we.
   Let all within us praise His holy name.

Chorus Christ is the Lord, oh praise His name forever!
   His pow'r and glory evermore proclaim!
   His pow'r and glory evermore proclaim!

O Leave Your Sheep

Traditional French Carol

Strum Pattern: 4
Pick Pattern: 3

Verse
Moderately

1. O leave your sheep, ye shep-herds come a-way, from
2. See additional lyrics

your flocks come, your sheep and lambs will stay. O

stop your tears, your souls with joy re-new. Come,

hur-ry to a-dore the One, the One, the

One who comes to com-fort you. 2. O herd.

Additional Lyrics

2. O see Him there, so tiny and so weak,
   A little babe within a manger laid.
   From heav'n above He comes the earth to save
   As God's incarnate word.
   He is, He is our Lord and our faithful shepherd.

O Little Town of Bethlehem

Words by Phillips Brooks
Music by Lewis H. Redner

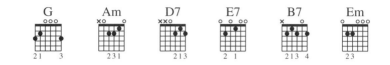

Strum Pattern: 4
Pick Pattern: 4, 5

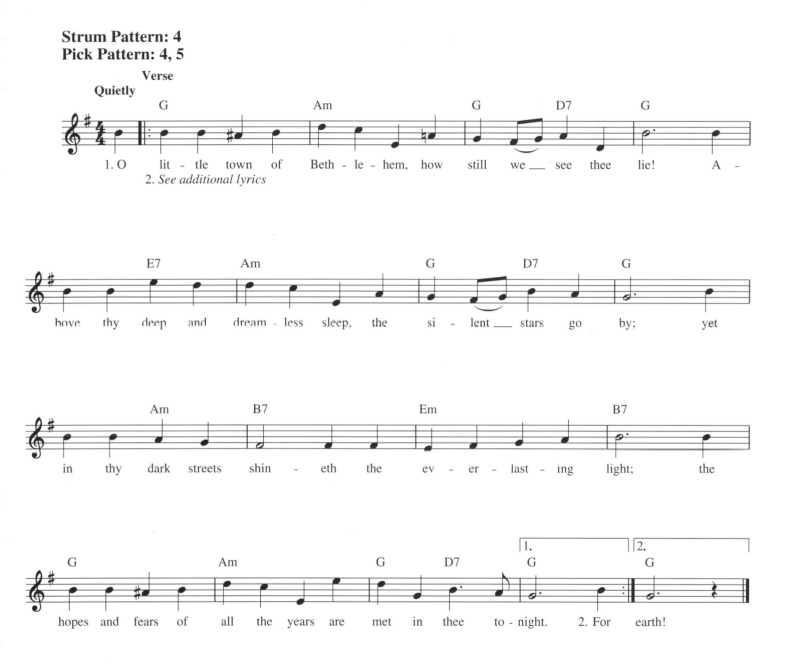

Additional Lyrics

2. For Christ is born of Mary, and gathered all above.
   While mortals sleep the angels keep
   Their watch of wond'ring love.
   O morning stars, together proclaim the holy birth!
   And praises sing to God the King,
   And peace to men on earth!

O Thou Joyful

Traditional German Carol

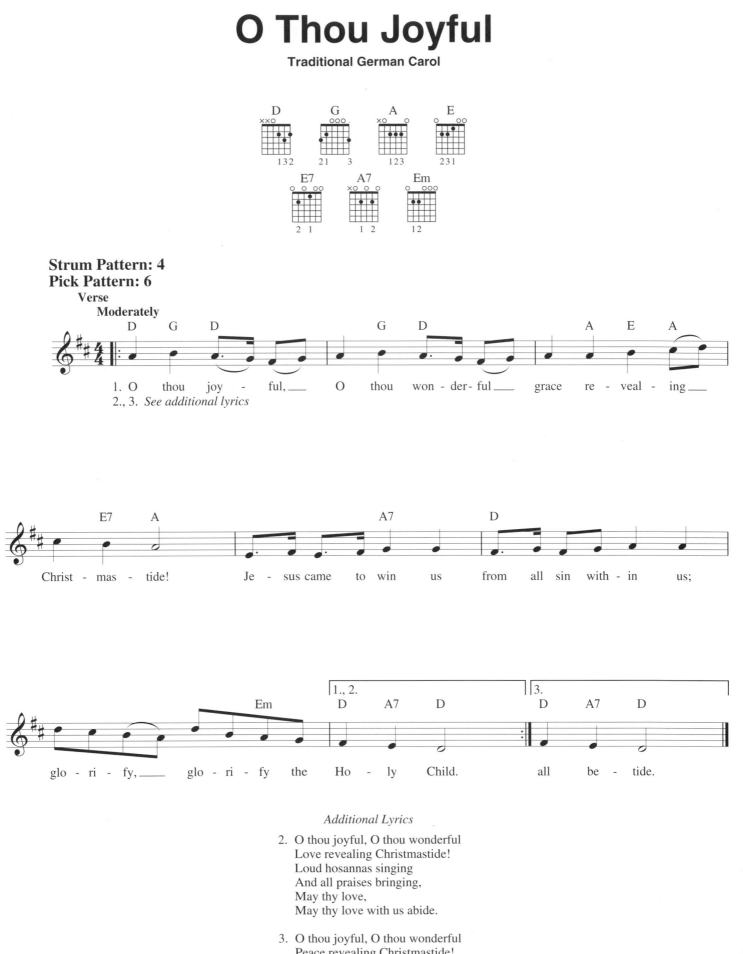

Additional Lyrics

2. O thou joyful, O thou wonderful
   Love revealing Christmastide!
   Loud hosannas singing
   And all praises bringing,
   May thy love,
   May thy love with us abide.

3. O thou joyful, O thou wonderful
   Peace revealing Christmastide!
   Darkness disappeareth,
   God's own light now neareth,
   Peace and joy,
   Peace and joy to all betide.

Oh! Dear Jesus

Traditional Italian Carol

Strum Pattern: 5
Pick Pattern: 4

Verse
Moderately

1. Thou cam-est from heav'n we are __ told, to keep God's prom-ise made of old.
2. *See additional lyrics*

His will was re-deem'd at Thy __ birth, thus we all wel-come Thee to earth.

Chorus

Oh! Dear Je - sus, sweet an-gel-ic child; __ Oh! Dear Je - sus, pre-cious Sav-ior mine; __

Oh! Dear Je - sus, Oh! Dear Je - sus, keep my love, it is ev - er Thine. ev - er Thine.

Additional Lyrics

2. Thy pilgrimage through starry skies,
   We greet with hosannas loud rise!
   God's love made manifest to men,
   For God His only Son hath giv'n.

Oh! Infant Jesus

Traditional Italian Carol

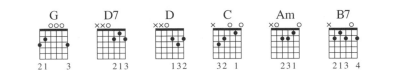

Strum Pattern: 7
Pick Pattern: 7

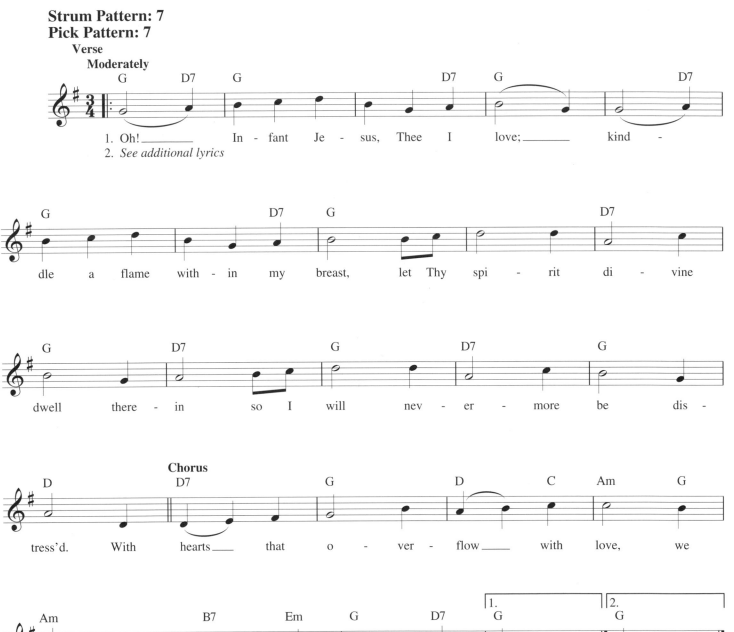

Additional Lyrics

2. Oh! Holy Infant, Thee I love;
   Be kind to all who dwell on earth,
   Child of grace, to Thee I humbly pray
   While I kneel and marvel at Your birth.

Once in Royal David's City

Words by Cecil F. Alexander
Music by Henry J. Gauntlett

Strum Pattern: 4
Pick Pattern: 5

Verse
Quietly

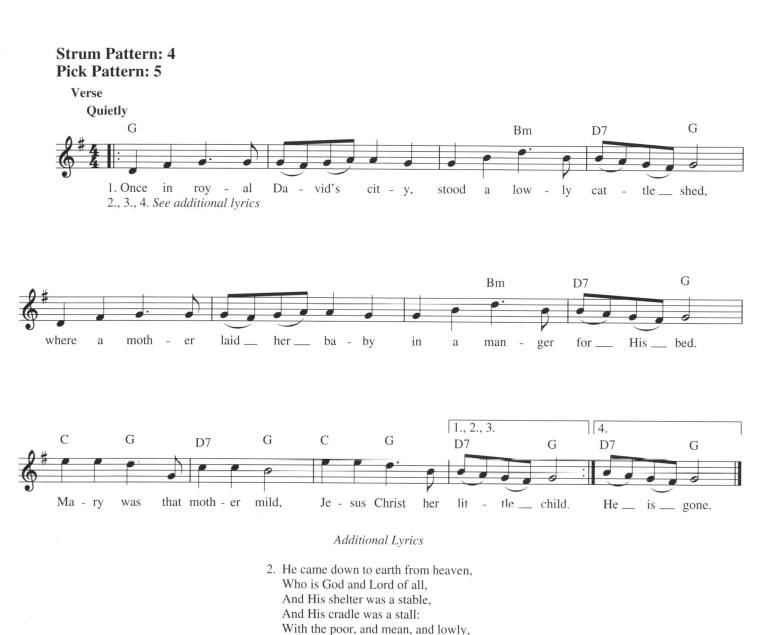

1. Once in roy - al Da - vid's cit - y, stood a low - ly cat - tle __ shed,
2., 3., 4. *See additional lyrics*

where a moth - er laid __ her __ ba - by in a man - ger for __ His __ bed.

Ma - ry was that moth - er mild, Je - sus Christ her lit - tle __ child. He __ is __ gone.

Additional Lyrics

2. He came down to earth from heaven,
   Who is God and Lord of all,
   And His shelter was a stable,
   And His cradle was a stall:
   With the poor, and mean, and lowly,
   Lived on earth our Savior holy.

3. Jesus is our childhood's pattern,
   Day by day like us He grew;
   He was little, weak and helpless,
   Tears and smiles like us He knew:
   And He feeleth for our sadness,
   And He shareth in our gladness.

4. And our eyes at last shall see Him,
   Through His own redeeming love.
   For that child so dear and gentle
   Is our Lord in heav'n above.
   And He leads His children on
   To the place where He is gone.

Pray, Give Us Lodging

Traditional Mexican Carol

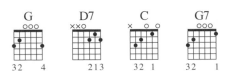

Strum Pattern: 9
Pick Pattern: 9

Verse
Moderately

1. *Joseph:* Pray give us lodg - ing dear, sir, in the name of heav'n,
2. – 6. *See additional lyrics*

all day since morn - ing to trav - el ____ we're ____ giv'n.

Ma - ry, my wife, is ex - pect - ing a child; she must have

re - fuge to - night. Let ____ us ____ in! Let ____ us ____ in! in!

Additional Lyrics

2. *Host:* You cannot stop here, I won't make my home an inn;
   I do not trust you, your story is thin.
   You two might rob me and then run away,
   Find somewhere else you can stay.
   Go away! Go away!

3. *Joseph:* Please show us pity! Your heart cannot be this cold!
   Look at poor Mary, so worn and so tired!
   We are most poor, but I'll pay what I can;
   God will reward you good man!
   Let us in! Let us in!

4. *Host:* You try my patience! I'm tired and must get some rest;
   I've told you kindly, but still you insist.
   If you don't go and stop bothering me,
   I'll fix you, I guarantee!
   Go away! Go away!

5. *Joseph:* Sir, I must tell you, my wife is the Queen of heaven,
   Chosen by God to deliver His Son.
   Jesus is coming to earth late this eve;
   (O heaven, make him believe!)
   Let us in! Let us in!

6. *Host:* Joseph, dear Joseph! O how could I be so blind?
   Not to know you and the Virgin so fine!
   Enter, blest trav'lers, my house is your own;
   Praise be to God on His throne!
   Please come in! Please come in!

Rejoice and Be Merry

Gallery Carol

Strum Pattern: 7
Pick Pattern: 7

Brightly

Re - joice and be mer - ry in songs and in mirth! O praise our Re -

deem - er, all mor - tals on earth! For this is the birth - day of

Je - sus our King, who brought us sal - va - tion His prais - es we'll sing!

Sing We Now of Christmas

Traditional

Strum Pattern: 3, 4
Pick Pattern: 3, 4

Joyfully

Sing we now of Christ - mas, No - el ___ sing we here. Sing our grate - ful

prais - es to the ___ maid so dear. Sing we No - el! The

King is born, No - el! Sing we now of Christ - mas, sing we ___ here No - el.

Ring Out, Ye Wild and Merry Bells

Words and Music by C. Maitland

Strum Pattern: 8
Pick Pattern: 8

Additional Lyrics

2. Ring out, ye silv'ry bells, ring out.
   Bring out your exultation
   That God with man is reconciled.
   Go tell it to the nations!
   Therefore let us all today,
   Glory in the highest!
   Banish sorrow far away,
   Glory in the highest!

Ring, Little Bells

Words by Karl Enslin
Traditional German Carol

Strum Pattern: 10
Pick Pattern: 10

Additional Lyrics

2. Maid and Infant tender,
Will you let us enter?
To us shelter giving
And the Child praising?

3. In our hearts now stealing,
Happiness the feeling,
Joy and blessing holy
From the Child so lowly.

Rise Up, Shepherd, and Follow

African-American Spiritual

Strum Pattern: 3
Pick Pattern: 3

Rocking

Traditional Czech Carol

Silent Night

Words by Joseph Mohr
Translated by John F. Young
Music by Franz X. Gruber

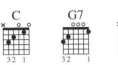

Strum Pattern: 7
Pick Pattern: 9

Additional Lyrics

2. Silent night, holy night!
   Shepherds quake at the sight.
   Glories stream from heaven afar.
   Heavenly hosts sing Alleluia.
   Christ the Savior is born!
   Christ the Savior is born!

3. Silent night, holy night!
   Son of God, love's pure light.
   Radiant beams from thy holy face
   With the dawn of redeeming grace,
   Jesus Lord at Thy birth.
   Jesus Lord at Thy birth.

The Simple Birth

Traditional Flemish Carol

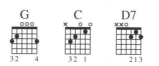

Strum Pattern: 8
Pick Pattern: 8

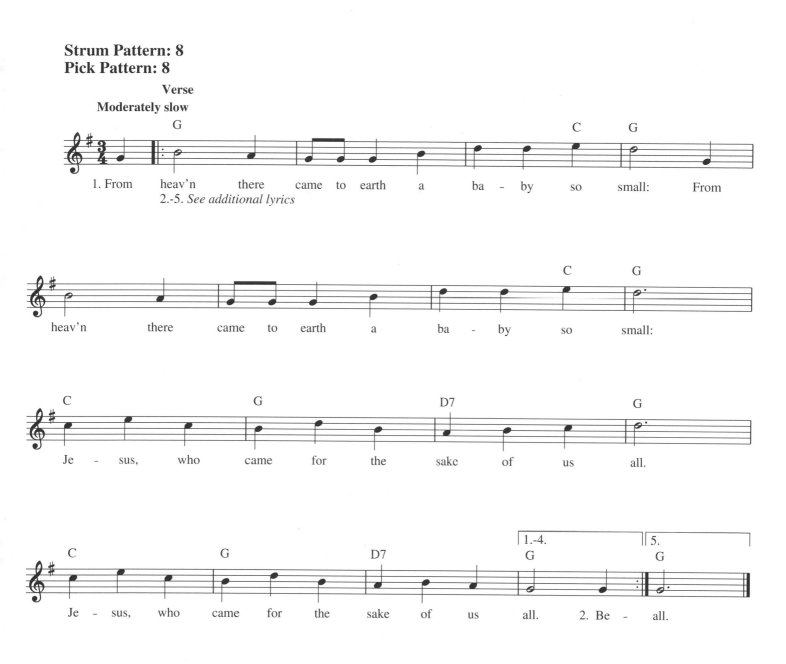

Additional Lyrics

2. Beneath His tiny head no pillow but hay:
   Beneath His tiny head no pillow but hay:
   God's richest treasures in rude manger lay.
   God's richest treasures in rude manger lay.

3. His eyes of blackest jet were sparkling with light:
   His eyes of blackest jet were sparkling with light:
   Rosy cheeks bloomed on His face fair and bright.
   Rosy cheeks bloomed on His face fair and bright.

4. And from His lovely mouth, the laughter did swell:
   And from His lovely mouth, the laughter did swell:
   When He saw Mary, whom He loved so well.
   When He saw Mary, whom He loved so well.

5. He came to weary earth, so dark and so drear:
   He came to weary earth, so dark and so drear:
   To wish to mankind a blessed New Year.
   To wish to mankind a blessed New Year.

Sleep, O Sleep, My Precious Child

Traditional Italian Carol

Strum Pattern: 10
Pick Pattern: 10

Additional Lyrics

2. O my darling, do not weep!
   Sweetly sleep, sweetly sleep,
   Close your eyes my Son, my dear one.
   Sweetly sleep, sweetly sleep.
   Close your eyes, my Son, my dear one.

The Sleep of the Infant Jesus

Traditional French Carol

Strum Pattern: 10
Pick Pattern: 10

Verse
Moderately

1. Here, 'mid the ass and ox - en mild,
2., 3. *See additional lyrics*

sleep, sleep, sleep, thou ti - ny Child.

Chorus

Thou - sand che - ru - bim, thou - sand ser - a - phim

guard - ing o'er the bed of the great Lord of love. love.

Additional Lyrics

2. Here, 'mid the rose and lily bright,
Sleep, sleep, sleep, thou tiny Child.

3. Here 'mid the shepherds' glad delight,
Sleep, sleep, sleep, thou tiny Child.

The Snow Lay on the Ground

Traditional Irish Carol

Strum Pattern: 7
Pick Pattern: 9

Verse

Slowly

1. The snow lay on the ground, the star shone bright when
2., 3. *See additional lyrics*

Christ our Lord was born on Christ - mas night. Ve - ni - te ad - o -

re - mus Do - mi - num; Ve - ni - te ad - o - re - mus

Chorus

Do - mi - num. Ve - ni - te ad - o - re - mus Do - mi -

num; Ve - ni - te ad - o - re - mus Do - mi - num. 2. 'Twas num.

Additional Lyrics

2. 'Twas Mary, virgin pure of Holy Anne
   That brought into this world the God-made man.
   She laid Him in a stall at Bethlehem.
   The ass and oxen share the roof with them.

3. Saint Joseph too, was by to tend the Child,
   To guard Him and protect His mother mild.
   The angels hovered 'round and sang this song;
   Venite adoremus Dominum.

The Son of Mary

Traditional Catalonian Carol

Strum Pattern: 8
Pick Pattern: 8

Verse
Moderately

1. What shall we give to the Son of the Vir - gin? What can we give that the

2., 3. *See additional lyrics*

Child will en - joy? First, we shall give Him a tray full of rai - sins,

then we shall of - fer sweet figs to the Boy. First, we shall give Him a

tray full of rai - sins, then we shall of - fer sweet figs to the Boy. figs will be seen.

Additional Lyrics

2. What shall we give the Beloved of Mary?
What can we give to her wonderful Child?
Raisins and olives and nutmeats and honey,
Candy and figs and some cheese that is mild.
Raisins and olives and nutmeats and honey,
Candy and figs and some cheese that is mild.

3. What shall we do if the figs are not ripened?
What shall we do if the figs are still green?
We shall not cry if they're not ripe for Easter,
On a Palm Sunday, ripe figs will be seen.
We shall not cry if they're not ripe for Easter,
On a Palm Sunday, ripe figs will be seen.

Song of the Wise Men

Traditional Puerto Rican Carol

Strum Pattern: 3, 4
Pick Pattern: 3, 4

1. From a far-off home the Sav-ior we come seek-ing, us-ing as our
2., 3., 4. *See additional lyrics*

guide the star, so bright-ly beam-ing. Love-ly East-ern Star, that

tells us of God's great love, heav-en won-drous light O nev-er cease thy

shin-ing! Glo-ry in the high-est to the Son of heav-en,

and up-on the earth be peace and love to men._____ men._____

Additional Lyrics

2. Glowing gold I bring
   The newborn Child so holy,
   Token of His pow'r
   To reign above in glory.

3. Frankincense I bring
   The Child of God's own choosing,
   Token of our praise
   To heaven ever rising.

4. Bitter myrrh have I
   To give the tiny Jesus,
   Token of the pain
   That He will bear to save us.

Star of the East

Words by George Cooper
Music by Amanda Kennedy

Still, Still, Still

Salzburg Melody, c. 1819
Traditional Austrian Text

D   Bm   Em   A7

Strum Pattern: 4
Pick Pattern: 3

Verse
Moderately slow

D   Bm   Em   A7   D

1. Still, ___ still, ___ still, ___ to ___ sleep is ___ now His ___ will. On
2. Sleep, ___ sleep, ___ sleep, ___ while ___ we Thy ___ vi-gil ___ keep. And

A7   D   A7   D

Mar - y's ___ breast He rests in ___ slum - ber, while we ___ pray in end - less ___ num - ber,
an - gels ___ come from heav - en ___ sing - ing songs of ___ ju - bi - la - tion bring - ing

                          Bm   Em   A7   1. D   2. D

still, ___ still, ___ still, ___ to ___ sleep is ___ now His ___ will.   keep.
sleep, ___ sleep, ___ sleep, ___ while ___ we Thy ___ vi - gil ___

Today We Welcome a Tiny Child

Traditional 14th Century Dutch Carol

G   D   C   D7   Am   Bm   Cadd9

Strum Pattern: 7
Pick Pattern: 7

Verse
Moderately

G   D   G   C   G   D7   G   D   G

1. To - day we wel - come a ti - ny Child that pales the sun's bright shin - ing, our
2. *See additional lyrics*

D   Am   G   D   Bm   G Cadd9   C   G   D7   1. G   2. G

hope and joy, this In - fant mild, whom an - gels' songs are pro - claim - ing. 2. The   en.

Additional Lyrics

2. The stars that fill the radiant sky
   Announce the gift from heaven,
   While Mary adores her holy Child,
   That God the Father has given.

Susani

14th Century German Carol

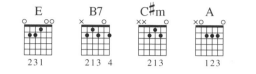

Strum Pattern: 7
Pick Pattern: 7

1. From heav-en on high, O an-gels sing! Ei -
2., 3., 4. *See additional lyrics*

a, ei - a! Su - sa - ni, su - sa - ni,

su - sa - ni! And let the joy - ful trum - pets

ring! Al - le - lu - ia! Al - le - lu - ia! Of

Ma - ry we sing,___ and Christ, her Son. 2. Come Son.

Additional Lyrics

2. Come bring your instruments so sweet!
   Eia, eia! Susani, susani, susani!
   With harp and chimes your Savior greet!

3. O lift your voices clear and high!
   Eia, eia! Susani, susani, susani!
   With strings and organ raise the cry!

4. Sing peace to all people far and wide!
   Eia, eia! Susani, susani, susani!
   And praise to God, our heav'nly guide!

Sussex Carol

Traditional English Carol

Strum Pattern: 8
Pick Pattern: 8

Verse
Brightly

1. On Christ-mas night, true Christ-ians sing, to hear the news the an-gels bring. On
3., 5., 7. *See additional lyrics*

Christ-mas night, true Christ-ians sing, to hear the news the an-gels bring.

Verse

2. News of great joy and of great mirth, ti-dings
4., 6., 8. *See additional lyrics*

of our dear Sav-ior's birth. 3. The

Additional Lyrics

3. The King of Kings to us is giv'n,
   The Lord of earth and King of heav'n.
   The King of Kings to us is giv'n,
   The Lord of earth and King of heav'n.

4. Angels and men with joy may sing
   Of blest Jesus, their Savior King.

5. So how on earth can men be sad,
   When Jesus comes to make us glad?
   So how on earth can men be sad,
   When Jesus comes to make us glad?

6. From all our sins to set us free,
   Buying for us our liberty.

7. From out the darkness have we light,
   Which makes the angels sing this night.
   From out the darkness have we light,
   Which makes the angels sing this night.

8. "Glory to God, His peace to men,
   And good will, evermore. Amen."

There's a Song in the Air

Words and Music by Josiah G. Holland and Karl P. Harrington

Strum Pattern: 7, 8
Pick Pattern: 8

Verse

Moderately

1. There's a song in the air! There's a star in the sky! There's a

2., 3., 4. *See additional lyrics*

moth - er's deep prayer and a ba - by's low cry! And the

star rains its fire while the beau - ti - ful sing, for the

man - ger of Beth - le - hem cra - dles a King! 2. There's a King!

Additional Lyrics

2. There's a tumult of joy o'er the wonderful birth,
   For the Virgin's sweet boy is the Lord of the earth.
   Ay! The star rains its fire while the beautiful sing,
   For the manger of Bethlehem cradles a King!

3. In the light of that star lie the ages impearled,
   And that song from afar has swept over the world.
   Ev'ry hearth is aflame, and the beautiful song,
   In the homes of the nations that Jesus is King!

4. We rejoice in the light, and we echo the song
   That comes down thro' the night from the heavenly throng.
   Ay! We shout to the lovely envangel they bring,
   And we greet in His cradle our Savior and King!

To Us Is Born a Little Child

Traditional German Carol

Strum Pattern: 8
Pick Pattern: 8

Verse
Moderately

1. To us is born ___ a lit - tle Child of Ma - ry,
2., 3. *See additional lyrics*

maid - en Moth - er mild, Yule - time a mer - ry

sea - son is, Babe Je - sus our de - light ___ and

Chorus

bliss. O Je - sus dar - ling of ___ my heart, ___ how

rich in mer - cy, Babe, ___ Thou art. art.

Additional Lyrics

2. Strange sight within a stable old,
   Lo, God is born in want and cold,
   O selfish world this Babe, I say,
   Doth put thee to the blush today.

3. Now angels joyful hymns upraise,
   And God's own Son with carols praise.
   To Bethlehem the shepherds fare,
   And firstlings of their flock they bear.

'Twas the Night Before Christmas

Words by Clement Clark Moore
Music by F. Henri Klickman

Strum Pattern: 4
Pick Pattern: 5

Verse

Brightly

1. 'Twas the night be-fore Christ-mas, when all through the house, not a crea-ture was stir-ring, not e-ven a mouse. The
2.-7. *See additional lyrics*

stock-ings were hung by the chim-ney with care, in hopes that Saint Nich-o-las soon would be there. The

chil-dren were nest-led all snug in their beds, while vis-ions of su-gar plums danced through their heads. And

Ma-ma in her 'ker-chief and I in my cap, had just set-tled our brains for a long win-ter's nap. 2. When all a good-night!"

Additional Lyrics

2. When out on the lawn there arouse such a clatter;
I sprang from my bed to see what was the matter.
Away to the window I flew like a flash,
Tore open the shutters and threw up the sash.
The moon, on the breast of the new-fallen snow,
Gave a lustre of midday to objects below.
When what to my wondering eyes should appear.
But a miniature sleigh and eight tiny reindeer.

3. With a little old driver; so lively and quick,
I knew in a moment it must be Saint Nick.
More rapid than eagles, his coursers they came
And he whistled, and shouted, and called them by name;
"Now, Dasher, Now, Dancer! Now, Prancer! Now, Vixen!
On Comet! On, Cupid! On Donder and Blitzen!
To the top of the porch, to the top of the wall!
Now dash away, dash away, dash away all!"

4. As dry leaves that before the wild hurricane fly,
When they meet with an obstacle, mount to the sky.
So up to the house-top the coursers they flew,
With the sleigh full of toys, and Saint Nicholas, too.
And then in a twinkling I heard on the roof
The prancing and pawing of each little hoof.
As I drew in my head, and was turning around,
Down the chimney Saint Nicholas came with a bound.

5. He was dressed all in fir from his head to his foot,
And his clothes were all tarnished with ashes and soot.
And he looked like a peddler just opening his pack.
His eyes how they twinkled! His dimples how merry!
His cheeks were like roses, his nose like a cherry,
His droll little mouth was drawn up like a bow
And the beard of his chin was as white as the snow.

6. The stump of a pipe he held tight in his teeth
And the smoke, it encircled his head like a wreath.
He had a broad face, and a round little belly
That shook, when he laughed, like a bowl full of jelly.
He was chubby and plump, a right jolly old elf,
And I laughed when I saw him, in spite of myself.
A wink of his eye and a twist of his head,
Soon gave me to know I had nothing to dread.

7. He spoke not a word but went straight to his work,
And filled all the stockings, then turned with a jerk,
And laying his finger aside of his nose,
And giving a nod, up the chimney he rose.
He sprang to his sleigh, to his team gave a whistle
And away they all flew like the down of a thistle,
But I heard him exclaim, ere he drove out of sight:
"Happy Christmas to all, and all a good-night!"

The Twelve Days of Christmas

Traditional English Carol

Up on the Housetop

Words and Music by B.R. Handy

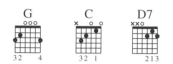

Strum Pattern: 4, 3
Pick Pattern: 4, 3

Additional Lyrics

2. First comes the stocking of Little Nell,
   Oh, dear Santa, fill it well.
   Give her a dollie that laughs and cries,
   One that will open and shut her eyes.

3. Next comes the stocking of little Will,
   Oh, just see what a glorious fill!
   Here is a hammer and lots of tacks,
   Also a ball and a whip that cracks.

Wassail Song

Traditional English Carol

*Strum Pattern: 10
*Pick Pattern: 10

Strum Pattern: 3
Pick Pattern: 3

Additional Lyrics

2. We are not daily beggars
   That beg from door to door.
   But we are neighbor children
   Whom you have seen before.

3. We have got a little purse
   Of stretching leather skin.
   We want a little money
   To line it well within:

4. God bless the master of this house,
   Likewise the mistress too;
   And all the little children
   That round the table go:

Watchman, Tell Us of the Night

Traditional

Strum Pattern: 4
Pick Pattern: 3

Verse
Moderately slow

1. Watch-man, tell us of the night, what its signs of prom-ise are.
2., 3. *See additional lyrics*

Trav-'ler, o'er yon moun-tain's height, see that glo-ry beam-ing star.

Watch-man, does __ its beau-teous ray aught of joy or hope for-tell?

Trav-'ler, yes, it brings the day, prom-ised day of Is-ra-el. God is come.

Additional Lyrics

2. Watchman, tell us of the night,
   Higher yet that star ascends.
   Trav'ler, blessedness and light,
   Peace and truth, its course portends.
   Watchman, will its beams alone
   Gild the spot that gave them birth!
   Trav'ler, ages are its own;
   See it bursts o'er all the earth.

3. Watchman, tell us of the night,
   For the morning seems to dawn.
   Trav'ler, darkness takes its flight;
   Doubt and terror are withdrawn.
   Watchman, let thy wanderings cease;
   Hie thee to thy quiet home!
   Trav'ler, lo, the Prince of Peace,
   Lo, the Son of God is come.

We Are Singing

Traditional Venezuelan Folk Carol

Strum Pattern: 4
Pick Pattern: 4

Chorus
Moderately

Sing - ing, we are sing - ing lov - ing praise we bring,

mer - ry eve of Christ - mas, mer - ry eve of Christ - mas,

mer - ry eve of Christ - mas, to Thee, In - fant King.

Fine

Verse

1. All our ex - pec - ta - tion, all our char - i - ty, _____
2., 3. *See additional lyrics*

all our con - so - la - tion, Child dear in Thee. love.

1., 2. **3.** **D.C. al Fine**

Additional Lyrics

2. Beaming through the darkness,
   Flooding rays so bright,
   Shining on the cradle,
   On the glorious night.

3. Night of celebration,
   Night of Jesus' birth,
   Night of holy splendor,
   And redeeming love.

We Three Kings of Orient Are

Words and Music by John H. Hopkins, Jr.

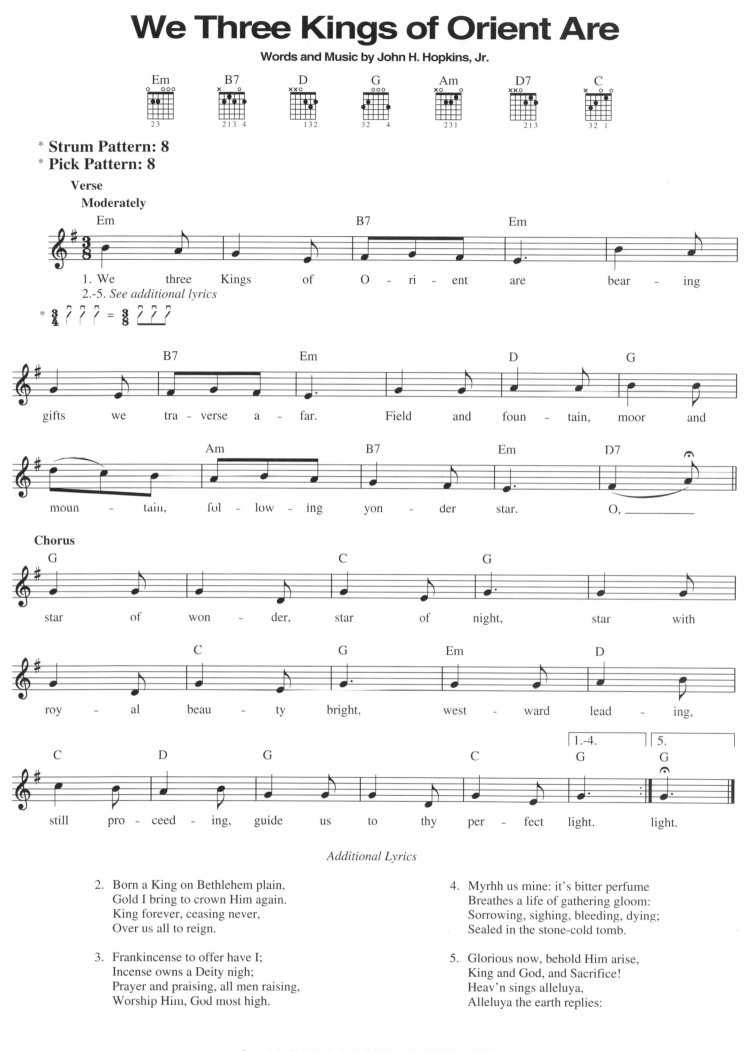

* **Strum Pattern: 8**
* **Pick Pattern: 8**

Verse
Moderately

1. We three Kings of O - ri - ent are bear - ing
2.-5. *See additional lyrics*

gifts we tra - verse a - far. Field and foun - tain, moor and

moun - tain, fol - low - ing yon - der star. O, _____

Chorus

star of won - der, star of night, star with

roy - al beau - ty bright, west - ward lead - ing,

still pro - ceed - ing, guide us to thy per - fect light. light.

Additional Lyrics

2. Born a King on Bethlehem plain,
Gold I bring to crown Him again.
King forever, ceasing never,
Over us all to reign.

3. Frankincense to offer have I;
Incense owns a Deity nigh;
Prayer and praising, all men raising,
Worship Him, God most high.

4. Myrhh us mine: it's bitter perfume
Breathes a life of gathering gloom:
Sorrowing, sighing, bleeding, dying;
Sealed in the stone-cold tomb.

5. Glorious now, behold Him arise,
King and God, and Sacrifice!
Heav'n sings alleluya,
Alleluya the earth replies:

We Wish You a Merry Christmas

Traditional English Folksong

Strum Pattern: 8, 9
Pick Pattern: 8, 9

Additional Lyrics

2. We all know that Santa's coming.
   We all know that Santa's coming.
   We all know that Santa's coming
   And soon will be here.

Welsh Carol

Words by Pastor K.E. Roberts
Traditional Welsh Carol

Am E7 Dm6 Dm G G7 C E

*Strum Pattern: 4
*Pick Pattern: 4

% Verse

Moderately

Am   E7   Am   E7   Am   Dm6   Dm   E7   Am   E7

1. A - wake were they on - ly, those shep - herds so lone - ly, on guard in that si -
light now en - fold us, O Lord, for be - hold us, like shep - herds from tu -

*Use Pattern 10 for 2/4 meas.

Am E7   Am   E7   Am   E7   Am   E7   Am   Dm6   Dm   E7

lence pro - found, when co - lor had fad - ed, when night - time had shad - ed their
mult with - drawn, nor hear - ing, nor see - ing, all oth - er care flee - ing, we

Am   E7   Am E7   Am   **Chorus** G   G7   C   G   Am   E   Am

sens - es from sight and from sound. Lo, 1., 3. then broke a won - der, then drift - ed a - sun -
wait the in - eff - a - ble dawn. Lo, 2., 4. Spir - it all - know - ing, thou source o - ver - flow -

E   Am   E Am   Dm6 Am   E   Am   E7 Am   E7 Am   Dm6

der the veils from the splen - dor of God, when light from the Ho - ly, came down to the low -
ing, O move in the dark - ness a - round, that sight may be in us, true hear - ing to win

4th time, To Coda ⊕ 1.   2. ***D.S. al Coda***
(take repeat)   ⊕ **Coda**

Dm   E7   Am   E7   Am E7   Am   G   G7   Am   Am

ly, and heav'n to the earth that they trod. O, found. 2. May   found.
us, glad tid - ings where Christ may be

Wexford Carol

Traditional Irish Carol

Strum Pattern: 7
Pick Pattern: 7

Verse
Moderately

1. Good peo - ple all this Christ-mas time, con - si - der well and
2., 3., 4., 5. *See additional lyrics*

bear in mind, what our good God for us has done, in send - ing His be -

love - ed Son. With Ma - ry ho - ly we should pray to God with love this

Christ - mas Day. In Beth - le - hem, up - on that morn, there

was a bless - ed Mes - si - ah born. 2. The in - cense sweet.

Additional Lyrics

2. The night before that happy tide,
   The noble Virgin and her guide,
   Were long time seeking up and down,
   To find a lodging in the town.
   But mark how all things came to pass,
   From ev'ry door repell'd alas!
   As long foretold, their refuge all,
   Was but an humble ox's stall.

3. Near Bethlehem did shepherds keep,
   Their flocks of lambs and feeding sheep,
   To whom God's angels did appear,
   Which put the shepherds in great fear.
   "Prepare and go," the angels said,
   "To Bethlehem, be not afraid,
   For there you'll find, this happy morn,
   A princely Babe, sweet Jesus born."

4. With thankful heart and joyful mind,
   The shepherds went the Babe to find,
   And as God's angel had foretold,
   They did our Savior Christ behold.
   Within a manger He was laid,
   And by His side the virgin maid,
   Attending on the Lord of life,
   Who came on earth to end all strife.

5. There were three wise men from afar
   Directed by a glorious star,
   And on they wandered night and day,
   Until they came where Jesus lay.
   And when they came unto that place,
   Where our beloved Messiah was,
   They humbly cast them at His feet,
   With gifts of gold and incense sweet.

What Child Is This?

Words by William C. Dix
16th Century English Melody

Strum Pattern: 8, 7
Pick Pattern: 8, 9

Additional Lyrics

2. So bring Him incense, gold and myrrh,
   Come peasant king to own Him;
   The King of kings salvation brings.
   Let loving hearts enthrone Him,

Chorus   Raise, raise the song on high,
   The Virgin sings her lullaby;
   Joy, joy for Christ is born,
   The Babe, the Son of Mary.

What Is This Fragrance So Appealing?

Traditional French Carol

Strum Pattern: 7
Pick Pattern: 7

Additional Lyrics

2. What is this star with brilliance shining
   Deep in the dark that blinds our sight?
   Never did morning's sun come dawning
   With a more radiant, glorious light.
   What is this star with brilliance shining
   Deep in the dark that blinds our sight?

3. In Bethlehem, a simple manger,
   Is born to you a Savior King.
   Hurry to kneel beside His manger
   Your ardent praise and worship bring.
   In Bethlehem, a simple manger,
   Is born to you a Savior King.

When Christ Was Born of Mary Free

Traditional English Carol

Strum Pattern: 3, 4
Pick Pattern: 3, 4

1. When Christ was born of Ma - ry free, in Beth - le - hem that fair ci - ty,
2., 3. *See additional lyrics*

an - gels sang there with mirth and glee: "In ex - cel - sis glo - ri - a."

Chorus

In ex - cel - sis glo - ri - a, in ex - cel - sis glo - ri - a,

in ex - cel - sis glo - ri - a, in ex - cel - sis glo - ri - a. 2. The glo - ri - a.

Additional Lyrics

2. The King is come to save mankind,
   As in the scripture truths we find.
   Therefore this song we have in mind,
   "In excelsis gloria."

3. Then, dearest Lord, for Thy great grace,
   Grant us in bliss to see Thy face,
   Thee we may sing to Thy solace,
   "In excelsis gloria."

Whence Comes This Rush of Wings

Traditional French Carol

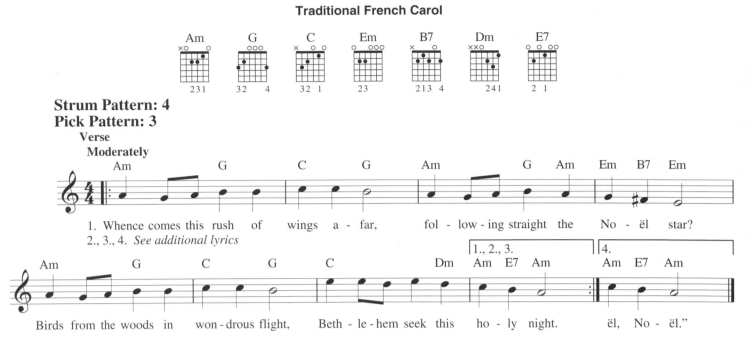

Strum Pattern: 4
Pick Pattern: 3

Verse
Moderately

1. Whence comes this rush of wings a - far, fol - low - ing straight the No - ël star?
2., 3., 4. *See additional lyrics*

Birds from the woods in won - drous flight, Beth - le - hem seek this ho - ly night.

ël, No - ël."

Additional Lyrics

2. "Tell us, ye birds, why come ye here,
Into this stable poor and drear?"
"Hast'ning we seek the newborn King,
And all our sweetest music bring."

3. Hark how the green finch bears his part,
Philomel, too, with tender heart
Chants from her leafy dark retreat,
"Re mi fa sol" in accents sweet.

4. Angels and shepherds, birds of the sky,
Come where the Son of God doth lie.
Christ on earth with man doth dwell,
Join in the shout, "Noël, Noël."

Yuletide Is Here Again

Traditional Swedish Dance Carol

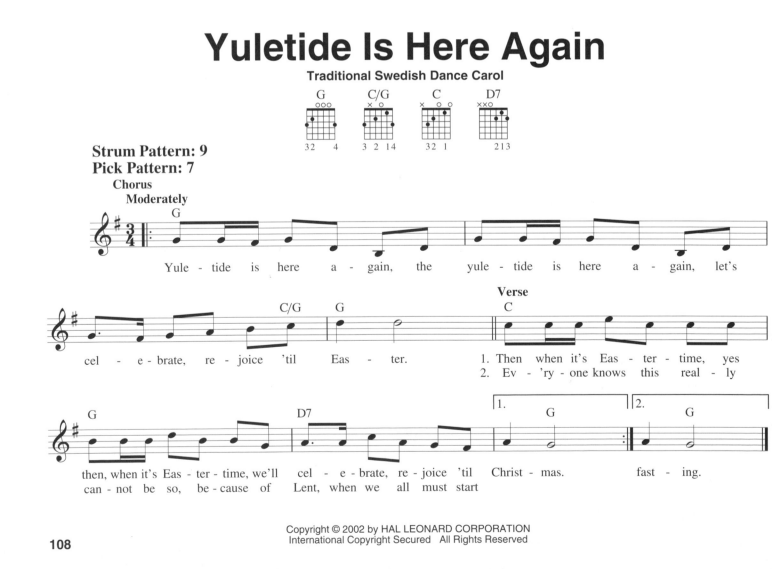

Strum Pattern: 9
Pick Pattern: 7

Chorus
Moderately

Yule - tide is here a - gain, the yule - tide is here a - gain, let's

cel - e - brate, re - joice 'til Eas - ter.

1. Then when it's Eas - ter - time, yes
2. Ev - 'ry - one knows this real - ly

then, when it's Eas - ter - time, we'll cel - e - brate, re - joice 'til Christ - mas.   fast - ing.
can - not be so, be - cause of Lent, when we all must start

While By My Sheep

Traditional German Carol

Strum Pattern: 4
Pick Pattern: 4

Additional Lyrics

2. There shall be born, so he did say,
   In Bethlehem, a Child today.

3. There shall He lie, in manger mean,
   Who shall redeem the world from sin.

4. Lord, evermore to me be nigh,
   Then shall my heart be filled with joy!

While Shepherds Watched Their Flocks

Words by Nahum Tate
Music by George Frideric Handel

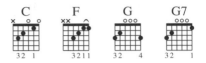

Strum Pattern: 3
Pick Pattern: 3

Additional Lyrics

2. "Fear not!" said he, for mighty dread
   Had seized their troubled mind.
   "Glad tidings of great joy I bring
   To you and all mankind,
   To you and all mankind.

3. "To you, in David's town this day,
   Is born of David's line,
   The Saviour, who is Christ the Lord;
   And this shall be the sign,
   And this shall be the sign:

4. "The heavenly Babe you there shall find
   To human view displayed,
   All meanly wrapped in swathing bands,
   And in a manger laid,
   And in a manger laid."

5. Thus spake the seraph; and forthwith
   Appeared a shining throng
   Of angels praising God on high,
   Who this addressed their song,
   Who this addressed their song.

6. "All glory be to God on high,
   And to the earth be peace;
   Good will henceforth from heaven to men,
   Begin and never cease,
   Begin and never cease!"

Ya Viene la Vieja

Traditional Spanish Carol

Strum Pattern: 8
Pick Pattern: 8

1. Come, my dear old wom - an, _____ with a lit - tle pres - ent, _____ that you love so dear - ly. _____ Of - fer it to Je - sus. We're weav - ing a gar - ment of green lem - on leaves, for sweet Vir - gin Ma - ry, the Moth - er of God! God!

2., 3. *See additional lyrics*

Additional Lyrics

2. Kings of Orient riding,
   Cross the sandy desert,
   Bringing to the Child,
   Wine and cookies sweet.

3. Kings of Orient riding,
   Guided by the starlight,
   Bringing to the Child,
   Gifts of love tonight.